From Ghetto to Death Camp

A Memoir of Privilege and Luck

ANATOL CHARI & TIMOTHY BRAATZ

The Disproportionate Press

Originally published in Germany as
Undermensch: Mein Überleben durch Glück und Privilegien
by Deutscher Taschenbuch Verlag, 2010

The Disproportionate Press

DP@lunycrab.com • www.lunycrab.com

FROM GHETTO TO DEATH CAMP

A MEMOIR OF PRIVILEGE AND LUCK

For my grandchildren Taco and Zoe.

In memory of all those mentioned in this book who, at one time or another, were responsible for my survival, especially Chaim Rumkowski; David Gertler; my friend and comrade Heniek Krakowski; Alfred, the French Häftling nurse at Wüstergiersdorf; and our compassionate German SS *Hauptscharführer* who treated prisoners like human beings—he was a decent man.

ACKNOWLEDGEMENTS

Two people deserve my special gratitude. Dr. Timothy Braatz was the motivating force behind this book. He encouraged me to share my wartime memories, and his careful questioning evoked incidents and details I thought I had forgotten. Put another way, it's his fault: he's the reason I went through the concentration camp experience—again. Dr. Andrea Wörle at DTV championed the manuscript and oversaw its original publication in Germany. I thank her for her enthusiasm, generosity, and especially her kindness.

- Anatol Chari

FROM GHETTO TO DEATH CAMP

A MEMOIR OF PRIVILEGE AND LUCK

INTRODUCTION

In 2001, I moved next door to Dr. Anatol "Tony" Chari in Laguna Beach, California, and we became friends. It's been tough duty. Not only have I had to sample old wine from his extensive collection, I've had to listen to his stories from World War II—another extensive collection. Double good fortune. As a student of history, concerned particularly with questions of violence and nonviolence, of human capacity to do good and to do horrible things, I was more than a little interested in his accounts of life in the Łódź ghetto and German concentration camps. On several occasions, Tony spoke to students in my Peace Studies course at Saddleback College. He started by describing his happiest, scariest, and saddest moments from the war, then pointed out the common element—all three were about food. In the ghetto and camps, he explained, that's all that really mattered. One time, I went with Tony when he spoke at an alternative high school. He was warned that the students, who had been expelled from other schools, might be restless and inattentive. To the contrary, his stories held them almost spellbound for an hour. Maybe, at some level, they could relate.

In 2007, we began to collaborate on this book. I listened again to his stories, this time taking notes and asking more questions. Tony emphasized one point above all else. He wanted it clear that he had survived the Holocaust because he was privileged. As he put it, "I didn't have it so bad." Through his father's connections, he became a *Sonderkommando* (Sonder, for short), a Jewish ghetto policeman, and this placed him in the ghetto's elite class. Not the super-elite, but, in a place where malnutrition led to many deaths, he was usually getting enough to eat. He had warm clothing, girlfriends, and his own apartment. And because of this, because he was healthier than most, he had a better chance of surviving the concentration camps after the ghetto was liquidated. To survive the camps, he now explains, you needed initiative, luck, and help—and then the chances still weren't good. In fact, you needed miracles. So his memoir is a story of privilege and luck.

However, this is not a memoir in the strictest sense of an individual writing a narrative of the past. Rather, it is a combination of memoir and oral history. This is Tony's story as told to me, as told through me, and some explanation is in order. In the decades after the war, Tony exchanged stories with fellow survivors, but didn't say too much to other acquaintances about his wartime experiences. Tony's public speaking career began around 1970, when his young daughter volunteered him to speak at her middle school. After the television series "The Holocaust" (1978) increased public interest, Tony received invitations to speak at synagogues and high schools. Sometime around 1990, Tony met a woman who offered to write his story. She interviewed him for two or three long days, produced sixty pages of rather amateurish prose on his years in the ghetto, then abandoned the project, telling him that his story had no value as a book. Tony was left with sixteen cassette tapes' worth of recorded interviews, which he paid someone else to transcribe. That transcript is one source for this present book. However, it is long, scattered, in some places unreadable, in others curiously interpreted. For example, Bergen-Belsen became "Berlin-Belgium," Hildesheim became "Hitlersan." The transcript does, however, hint at some tension between Tony and the interviewer. At one point, Tony was explaining how his block leader in Auschwitz had been a decent guy.

Tony: I've never seen him hit anybody. He had his underlings do the hitting, because there had to be a feeling of terror or whatever in the block. If not, the SS wouldn't have allowed him to be in charge.

Interviewer: Maybe he didn't do it directly but there was some hitting and he was responsible for it.

T: Look, don't try to put words in my mouth.

I: But you said that his underlings would.

T: It wasn't the same. When the guy in charge, like another block greener, hit you and beat you up it was as likely that you didn't survive as that you did. In his block there was no damage done.

It seems that Tony was trying to tell one story—about his privilege and relative good fortune—while she was searching for a different one, perhaps with greater emphasis on suffering and victimhood. This may explain why she didn't continue.

That's what I had to work with—an unsatisfactory oral history transcript and, of course, a live source. By nature, Tony is a storyteller. Over the years, he has fashioned a series of narratives—episodes, as it were, from his wartime experiences, including those tailored to student audiences. These episodes were in the transcript, I'd heard them on multiple occasions, and they were remarkably consistent. He had his stories and was sticking to them. Collectively, they insisted on a nuanced understanding of human behavior in extreme circumstances. This was not a world of moral absolutes. Tony survived because he had it better than others. Anyone who survived had it better than others. Theft was necessary for survival. Stealing from the common pot wasn't stealing, it was "organizing." Not all Germans were bad. Some guards were decent people. Some prisoners were not. My task, as I understood it, was not to find answers to specific historical questions, but, rather, to assemble Tony's set pieces in an accessible, readable form, while preserving his themes, delivering his message. In our interview sessions, I prodded Tony to clarify and elaborate, to offer more of a timeline, to fill in the blanks. So now there were two minds, two agendas, at work. Tony wanted to tell a certain story. I wanted to give it a certain shape. How does one evaluate the result?

Memory is a funny thing. It is constantly being reinvented. Eyewitnesses are notoriously unreliable. What, then, to make of an old survivor's account of what happened to him over sixty years ago, as filtered through the mind and pen of a much younger historian with his own strong views of the world and the past? In our sessions, Tony would sometimes warn, "There's no way you can understand what it was like if you weren't there. I *was* there, and I don't understand what it was like." So much time had passed that he couldn't always relate to the experiences he was describing. "Can you imagine," he would ask, almost mystified, "being so focused on food?" And yet some moments—like the last time he saw his father or when he looked into a rifle barrel as a German guard threatened to shoot him— were still fresh in his mind. "I can see it like it was yesterday," he said. What can be trusted? This is not a day-by-day diary, written in the heat (or bone-chilling cold) of the moment, like Dawid Sierakowiak's invaluable notebooks from the Łódź ghetto. Nor is it a testimony written within a few years of the war, when the memories, rightly or wrongly, might be considered more reliable, more "truthful." Undoubtedly, Tony has chosen to remember some things and forget others. The stories he did retain, we have to assume, have been shaped by his experiences and evolving mind over the decades. They have been informed by extensive reading in Holocaust history. Ask him if he thinks about the Holocaust often, and he'll reply, "Not often. Constantly." His brain has not stood still, and the reader should beware.

It seems worth noting that Tony is straightforward when recounting his past. He gives little impression of wanting to avoid certain topics or hide certain details, the exception being his hesitation to mention the last names of certain individuals. "I don't want to speak bad of the dead," he says. He doesn't shy away from discussing sexual encounters in the ghetto or his role as a Jewish policeman. He says he knows other former Sonders who have never told anybody, not even their children, about their controversial occupation in the ghetto. In fact, there are very few known testimonies from ghetto policemen, which makes Tony's recollections all the more valuable. Ghetto policemen were resented by other ghetto residents for their privilege, in particular their access to food, and their cooperation with German authorities. Tony has opinions on this, but does not deny his role. Tony speaks with an emotional detachment—perhaps a function of his distance from the events, though he says that he never learned to hate. He may disagree, but I think the stories he tells suggest he has pondered for years the reasons he survived and others didn't. For him, this is less a religious or philosophical question—he's not one for much philosophizing—and more a historical or even scientific one. He's a doctor by training, after all. The result is a matter-of-fact narration that some might fault for downplaying suffering and blame, for being too forgiving of some German participants. "This is my experience," Tony wants it understood. "Others may have had different experiences, but this is how it was for me."

I'm not a Holocaust scholar. I turned to reading secondary source material on the Holocaust only after having written a satisfactory draft of Tony's story. My research was mostly concerned with the timeline; I wanted to include a few verifiable dates as mileposts for the reader. And, of course, my curiosity was piqued. In examining studies of the Jewish ghettos, concentration camps, and the war, I found no reason to distrust Tony's voice. Despite a few internal inconsistencies—or perhaps strengthened by them— his stories rang true. Where verifiable, the facts generally checked out. Of particular interest is Sierakowiak's account of the Łódź ghetto, which Tony read for the first time only recently. Sierakowiak's description of the socioeconomic structures in the ghetto closely matches Tony's version, only Sierakowiak was writing from outside the privileged class. Taken together, Sierakowiak's agonizing deprivation and condemnation of the elite classes and Tony's time-tempered confessions of a privileged Sonder reveal a society where the accident of birth, access to education, and vagaries of chance meant the difference between a short, miserable existence and a more desirable life—a microcosm of our global society, it seems to me.

Tony has carefully and repeatedly read, edited, and suggested changes to what I have put down on paper. We both have added a few details, like the occasional statistic, from secondary sources to provide the non-expert reader with a modicum of historical context. His stories, though, remain almost word-for-word. I'm also a playwright, and I hope I've succeeded at selecting and arranging Tony's phrases in a way that preserves his character, especially his ironic humor, love of wordplay, and sometimes stubborn opinions. People who know me may interpret these as my voice creeping in, but he's like that too, I swear! That's why we're such good friends. We do, though, have a disagreement about the final chapter. The story that Tony wanted to tell—his life in the ghetto and camps—ended with his liberation from Bergen-Belsen. For him, Chapter 6 is not of great interest. I think his stories from the period immediately after the war, when he was a Displaced Person under British and American authority, are no less interesting and worth including. It is likely that readers have some knowledge of the camps but know little about life in occupied Germany.

One historical detail may bring confusion. All the published accounts I looked at agree that Bergen-Belsen was liberated on April 15, 1945, when British forces entered the camp and, using loudspeakers mounted on an armored vehicle, announced "You are free" to thousands of inmates. Tony remembers something different. He insists that ambulances—vans with red crosses painted on the side—drove down the main road of the camp and announced, "You are now under the protection of the International Red Cross." According to published accounts, the Royal Army Medical Corps arrived on April 17 and the British Red Cross on April 23. Does Tony remember correctly? Perhaps there were several different moments of liberation. Bergen-Belsen was actually several camps, British and German forces were engaged in heavy combat nearby on April 13 and 14, it was not an orderly scene. Perhaps he has conflated several different events. One thing is certain: Tony believes he saw ambulances and heard the words

"International Red Cross." That's his experience, that's what he remembers. Who am I to argue?

-Timothy Braatz

PROLOGUE

There is a right way and a wrong way to pull a corpse. That's what I learned at Bergen-Belsen. That's all you did at Bergen-Belsen—pull corpses. There was nothing else to do. It was four prisoners to a corpse. You grabbed an arm or a leg, you tied a belt or piece of string to the wrist or ankle, and you always pulled feet first. If you pulled head first, you lifted the upper body off the ground. The head would bob up and down and the legs, dragging behind, would spread wide, making the pulling more difficult. If you pulled feet first, the body would be flat on the ground and drag smoothly. The guys pulling the arms would be two steps behind you. The head came last. You dragged the corpse a half mile or so to the pit, a mass grave, and tossed it in. Then you walked back to camp for another one. There were corpses everywhere. It didn't matter much which you chose. They were all emaciated and weighed next to nothing. We dragged them from where they dropped. One time we were pulling a corpse, and one guy said he was tired and needed to rest for a few minutes. Soon we were pulling him. It was total exhaustion. There was nothing left. Just the spirit and bone and skin. No muscle. If the spirit still pulled, that was fine. If the spirit gave out, that was the end of it.

I had been at Auschwitz. That was a good camp to be in, as concentration camps go. You had work. Maybe you dug ditches or you unloaded trains. You had the pretense that you were useful. They might let you live. And if not, at least you died cleanly—to the gas chamber and the crematorium, up the chimney, and that was it. Bergen-Belsen was a bad camp. Nothing to eat. Dirty clothing crawling with typhoid-carrying lice.

No pretense of usefulness. The first thing you lost in Bergen-Belsen was hope. And death was an installment plan. It was suffered. Every day a little bit more. You just waited to die. One night I used a corpse for a pillow. What did he care? That was Bergen-Belsen. Nothing but dirt, suffering, and corpses. Thousands of walking corpses dragging thousands of lifeless corpses. We pulled corpses the whole time I was there—ten days, or maybe fourteen, I don't remember exactly. I wouldn't have lasted much longer. There was no hope. Then the British liberated us. April 15, 1945. That was the end of the war for me. It had begun over five and a half years earlier. Five and a half lost years. This is the story of how I survived.

1

MY FATHER'S COATTAILS

The German army invaded Poland on September 1, 1939, and a few days later they reached Łódź, a big, dirty, industrial town, the second largest city in Poland.[1] I was sixteen. I lived in Łódź with my father and stepmother. We knew the invasion wouldn't be good for us. Already there was a refugee camp at Zbąszyń, near the German border, for eastern European Jews evicted from Germany a year earlier, so we knew something about the German government's attitude toward Jews. Poland, of course, had its anti-Jewish practices. For example, Jewish children had difficulty getting into public gymnasiums, and universities had quotas on Jewish students.[2] But nobody knew how bad it would become. The day the Germans arrived, there was a commotion in the street—probably military vehicles moving into the center of town. We were too scared to go outside and see. That evening, local ethnic Germans—*Volksdeutsche*—marched in the streets, celebrating and saluting Hitler. Within a few days, we were hearing stories about Germans grabbing Jews in the street and humiliating them. Some were beaten. Some were forced to clean stairs in military barracks with a toothbrush. We saw Orthodox Jews with their sidelocks and beards cut off.

My father, Piotr Chari, thought maybe we should flee to eastern Poland—Belarussia—where he was born. Of course, that area was now under Russian occupation, and, as Father pointed out, in Łódź at least we had

---

[1] The German army occupied Łódź on September 8. The city, a major textile center, was home to around 750,000 people, one third of them Jews. Lucjan Dobroszycki, ed., *The Chronicle of the Łódź Ghetto 1941-1944* (New Haven: Yale University Press, 1984), xxx.
[2] A gymnasium is a high school. Most Jewish students went to private Jewish gymnasiums.

a bed to sleep in. Go or stay? Neither choice looked good, but the Germans didn't wait for Father to make up his mind. They were rounding up city leaders, university professors—anyone influential who might organize some kind of resistance—and Father was well-known. He owned two apartment buildings and a dry goods store. He was on the inner board of the Łódź chamber of commerce and industry, and he was on the Jewish city council, the *kehillah*, which attended to the concerns of the Łódź Jews.[3] On November 10—that date I remember—two Gestapo men came to our apartment. One spoke fluent Polish, and asked for Councilman Chari. He didn't say, "Where's the Jew Chari?" They were polite.

"He's not at home," my stepmother told them.

"When do you expect him?"

"I don't know."

So they took me instead. They said they would hold me until Father showed up at the office of a Jewish small business organization where he served as chairman. Father was somewhere in the apartment building, and he saw them taking me out, but he didn't come for an hour. Probably he changed clothes. I know he put on a warm coat. He couldn't be sure how long he would be gone. I was just sitting there waiting. The Gestapo men asked, "Where do you think he is?" I told them I had no idea. When Father finally arrived at the office, he was standing in the outer hallway. I tried to walk over and kiss him, say goodbye. But he just said, "Go home. I'll be back soon." Perhaps he thought they just wanted to ask him some questions. In my mind, I can still see him standing in that hallway, telling me to go home. I never saw him again.

The day before, the Germans had opened a prison at Radogoszcz, outside Łódź, for political arrests, and Father was taken there.[4] Every day for two weeks, my aunt Sarah rode the streetcar to the prison to take him food. One day she was told, "He isn't here anymore." That was the last we heard. But I kept thinking he would return, hoping he would return. I had to go on living my life, waking up each day, even with Father missing, and it helped to

---

[3] In the 1930s, the Jewish population of Łódź "fluctuated between 230,000 and 250,000." Dobroszycki, *The Chronicle*, xxxviii.

[4] On November 10, 1939, "all the members of the Jewish city council have been imprisoned." Dawid Sierakowiak, *The Diary of Dawid Sierakowiak: Five Notebooks from the Lodz Ghetto* (New York: Oxford University Press, 1996), 61. According to Isaiah Trunk, *Łódź Ghetto: A History* (Bloomington: Indiana University Press, 2006), 34, "all were sent to…Radogoszcz (Radegast), where some were murdered by shooting and torture and five members were deported to Kraków in December."

have hope. No one told me that the last time Sarah saw him, he looked pretty bad. That I learned from my cousin Chaim only recently.

Unfortunately, the Germans were making it clear that life would not remain normal. Our apartment was on Piotrkowska, the main street of Łódź. The Germans renamed the street Adolf Hitler Strasse and declared it off-limits to Jews.[5] I was still going to Schweitzer Gymnasium, a private Jewish high school, so I had to run across the street to a large apartment building with a courtyard where we sometimes played soccer. I could cross the courtyard and exit onto another street and go to school. The Germans imposed a curfew on the entire city. After five in the evening, you were not permitted outside. You were supposed to surrender your radio if you had one. I spent the evenings playing cards with the neighbors. There was little else to do. Also, the Germans announced that all Jews had to wear a yellow armband. You had to comply. It was punishable by death. You could be shot on the spot. Jews had no protection. We were fair game. But if you carried a coat or a blanket, and placed it to cover the armband, you could cross the street or go somewhere forbidden to Jews without being noticed.

The German soldiers began stealing from us. A couple of soldiers went into my Aunt Fela's leather goods store. They used old German marks, revoked and worthless, to "buy" some of the fancier items, and wouldn't take no for an answer. A soldier came into our apartment and saw my fancy bicycle in the hallway. "I want it and I will have it," he said. He came back the next day and took it. In our apartment building, there was a warehouse which held cotton and other raw materials for the textile factories. German soldiers drove up in a truck and started looting the warehouse. The owner ran to the German military commandant to complain. A general showed up and stopped the looting. However, within a week, the man who complained was arrested and never seen again.

Next, the Germans ordered all Jewish residents of Adolf Hitler Strasse to relocate. There were two nights of terror. SS men went into two large apartment buildings, called out the inhabitants, and beat people up. They killed a few children by slamming their heads against the wall. Within two days, there were no Jews living on our street. My stepmother moved in with her sister, who lived in a small apartment with her husband and two sons. I

---

[5] The announcement was posted in Łódź on November 7, 1940. Sierakowiak, *The Diary*, 60. Germans renamed all Łódź streets and squares, banned the Polish language in schools, and even renamed the city Litzmannstadt as part of a policy of Germanizing annexed territory. Dobroszycki, *The Chronicle*, xxiii-xxiv.

decided to live with my maternal grandparents. My father's parents died before I was born. My parents divorced when I was two or three, and I had gone with my father, who remarried when I was around ten or twelve. I was never really on good terms with my mother. She was a strong-willed woman, a very successful high-class clothing designer, educated in Paris. She usually lived there or in Belgium or in Warsaw. I know I visited her once in Warsaw. Otherwise, I only saw her two or three times a year. I remember she would bring pineapples, a real delicacy in pre-war Poland. But I was close to her parents, closer than she was. My grandfather was a leatherworker. He once owned the biggest, most fashionable leather store in Łódź. He sold billfolds and suitcases and everything in between. The store went bankrupt during the 1930s depression, and Grandfather retired. He and my grandmother lived in a huge apartment on Narutowicza Street, about a twenty-minute walk from my school, and sometimes, if I had an extra period between classes, I would run to see Grandma. She would make an omelet for me. It was an unexpected pleasure for her to see her grandson. When the war began, my mother was in Łódź, staying with my grandparents. With Father gone, and my stepmother in a crowded place, I joined them. I didn't go alone. My mother discovered I had brought lice. It wasn't my fault. This was my first war, and I didn't realize that lice know when a war begins, but somehow they do. My mother boiled all my clothes, and the lice were gone. I would see them again.

The Germans weren't finished. One day, when I was home alone, a huge SS man came into our apartment, looked around, and began opening all the doors and drawers in the dining room sideboard. He had all the tools needed to open them, and he took whatever he wanted, including some of Grandfather's fancy crocodile-skin billfolds. He demanded I give him some paper, then he ripped a cord off the drapery, and wrapped up his treasure. Then he ordered me to clean up the room. He promised he would come back the next day to check on it. He didn't, but I was scared enough to obey.

Scared and cold. Winter was coming. Father was gone. The Germans destroyed the Łódź synagogues.[6] Blew them up. I remember wishing I could just go to sleep and wake up when the war was over. Then we had to move again. The poorest, dirtiest part of Łódź was the Jewish Quarter, called

---

[6] The Nazis burned the Reform Temple on the night of November 14-15 and the Old Town Synagogue the following night. Alan Adelson and Robert Lapides, eds., *Łódź Ghetto: Inside a Community under Siege* (New York: Viking, 1989), 69-71.

Bałuty. In December, word spread that the Germans were planning a Jewish ghetto. They would force the Polish residents of Bałuty and nearby neighborhoods to move out and all Łódź Jews to move in. Although thousands of Jews were fleeing the city, the ghetto would be extremely crowded and uninviting. The order to relocate came in February, 1940, and the Germans increased the terror to speed up the process, but my family had already moved.[7] It was first come, first served. You could make arrangements with Polish residents, perhaps pay a small bribe, to take over their house or apartment when they moved out. If not, the *Judenrat*, the Jewish Council selected by the Germans to administer the ghetto, would assign you a place to live. In January, my uncle Arek went to Bałuty and obtained a little house from a Polish family. We put a few belongings on a cart and moved there. I took practically nothing—a few shirts. When we were cleaning out the apartment, going through drawers, I found two old Cuban cigars from the time of World War I. The wrappers, the outer leaves, were so pale they were white. I smoked them. They were nothing like the cigarettes I smoked occasionally. The cigar smoke was soft and nice in the throat. I still remember that.

Our new home was a duplex—number 13 Wesoła Street—next to an old Jewish cemetery and a small insane asylum. Each side of the little house included one bedroom and a kitchen. On our side, my mother, grandparents, and I slept in the kitchen, a small room with a coal-burning stove. We put two beds along the length of one wall. I had a collapsible bed that we kept in a closet during the day. Between my bed, when it was down, and the door there was enough space for a small table about three fourths the size of a card table. That was it. You couldn't move around. The small bedroom next to us was for my mother's sister Eva, her husband Arek who had made the arrangements, his sister, her husband, and their two children, Mirka and Kuba. The Mak family lived in the bedroom and kitchen on the other side of the house. They included a father and mother, a daughter, two sons, the wife of one son, and perhaps a child. My mother's sister Fela had married a third son, Felek Mak. Those two were in a different Jewish ghetto, in Tomaszów, but as far as we were concerned, their marriage made the Maks our relatives.

---

[7] The ghetto plan was outlined in a secret German memorandum on December 8, 1939. The official order was announced on February 8, 1940. Trunk, *Łódź Ghetto*, 19-26. The ghetto, initially covering four square kilometers, included Bałuty, Stare Miasto (the Old Town), and the suburban area of Marysin. The Germans later reduced the area. Dobroszycki, *The Chronicle*, xxxvii.

We were all family, but this was not what we were used to. There was electricity, but no gas for cooking, no running water. We had an outhouse in our yard, but for well water we had to use the hand pump in the yard next door.[8] Of the sixteen or seventeen of us crammed into four small rooms, only nine would live through the war—and that was a pretty good survival rate for ghetto residents. There was one nice feature. Our little house was behind a large fence. You couldn't see it from the street. You could pretend it didn't exist. You could pretend *you* didn't exist.

We had a name for the Jews who already lived in Bałuty before the war. The *Volksdeutsche* were ethnic Germans born outside Germany. The *Reichsdeutsche* were Germans born in Germany, in the Reich. The latter considered themselves the better class of Germans. So we began calling the Bałuty Jews the *Reichsbałuter*. It was a joke, because anyone living in Bałuty before the war began—a native Bałuter—was definitely not the better class. But I made new friends among them, and we played cards by moonlight. And, almost every evening, I went to the insane asylum next door to visit the head nurse. She was a friend of my mother's youngest sister, Reginka. She was someone to talk to. Then the Germans took away all fifty or sixty asylum inmates on trucks. They went without protest. Someone told me that one inmate jumped off the truck and ran inside, then came back out with his violin. The Germans closed the asylum, and the nurse left, probably to Warsaw. I think that was around the end of February.[9] In the spring, one of my neighbors sold me her son's suit. She needed the money, and the brown suit fit me, so I bought it. I don't remember where I got the money, but I do know I was very proud of the suit. I hoped my father would see me wearing it. I still believed it was possible he would. But instead of seeing my father return that spring, I watched my mother depart.

The Germans surrounded the ghetto with a barbed-wire fence, and on May 1, 1940, they closed the gates. Before that, we could come and go, bring in more of our possessions. Now, we were sealed in, isolated from the outside world. In the Warsaw ghetto, the sewer tunnels allowed for contact beyond the walls, but Bałuty had no sewer system. We saw the lockdown

---

[8] According to German records, 164,000 Jews lived in 48,102 rooms, and only 725 apartments had running water. Adelson and Lapides, *Łódź Ghetto*, 58.

[9] Dobroszycki, *The Chronicle*, 67, n79, reports an asylum evacuation on Wesoła Street in March, 1940, and another in July, 1941. The patients were tranquilized to ensure an orderly removal. In both cases, all the patients deported from the ghetto were murdered in nearby forests by Germans.

Anatol Chari's maternal grandfather, Rafal Grabowiecki, on his summer estate in the 1920s, with his three daughters (from left, Irka, Anatol's mother Anna, and Eva) and two admirers

coming, and, on April 29 or 30, my mother announced that she and I were leaving. When the Germans invaded Poland, they annexed the western region, including Łódź, into the Reich as the Warthegau. They occupied and administered central Poland as a "protectorate," calling it the General Government.[10] My mother believed we would be safer in Warsaw, in the occupied territory, than under direct German rule in the Reich. She would pay someone to smuggle us out of Łódź before the ghetto was sealed, and then we would go northeast to Warsaw where her sister Irene lived. I told her, "In a burning building, it doesn't make much sense to move from one floor to the other." She left without me. If we had been closer, probably I would have gone with her. I don't know. I chose to stick it out in Łódź.

---

[10] German indecision, in autumn, 1939, over whether to allocate Łódź to the Reich or to the General Government delayed the eastward deportation of Łódź Jews and led, instead, to the ghettoization plan. The ghetto would hold the Jews until complete deportation out of the Warthegau could be arranged. Christopher Browning, *The Origins of the Final Solution: The Evolution of Nazi Jewish Policy, September 1939-March 1942* (Lincoln: University of Nebraska Press, 2004), 47-53, 113-114.

That proved to be a good decision. In 1942 and 1943, most of the Jews in the Warsaw ghetto were transported to Treblinka and gassed. I assume my mother and her sister were among them.

After my mother left, I stayed with my grandparents for about a month, then moved in with my father's sister's family. This was Aunt Rivka, her husband Jakob, and their three children, Lolek, Chaim, and Niusia. Before the war, they spent summer vacations in the countryside, renting a kitchen and a few rooms from a farmer, and I went with them. I was the rich cousin. I had a bicycle and always a ball for soccer or volleyball. But Chaim, a year and a half older, was my hero. Now, in the ghetto, all six of us were in one room. For a time, my uncle had a job distributing food to ghetto residents, so we could get a little bit extra to eat. The older cousin, Lolek, worked with the Jewish police. In the ghetto, we would say you can't take a piss on the side of a wooden house because before you finished someone would tear it apart for firewood. Everyone was looking for fuel. Lolek's job was guarding unoccupied buildings so they wouldn't become firewood.

Later, in 1941, Lolek's job was eliminated and the entire family was chosen to be "relocated." This was different from selections for extermination, which began in 1942. The Germans told the Jewish Council to provide a certain number—maybe several hundred or one thousand—for work. The council had to decide who would go.[11] When Lolek learned his family was included, he used his police connections to have them removed from the list. I was visiting them when he brought the news. He told the family, "You don't have to go. I'm the only one." At the time, we didn't think about extermination camps. We didn't know. The council mostly chose able-bodied men at this time, and the rumor in the ghetto was they were sent to Poznań for road work. In fact, two guys who escaped from Poznań were caught sneaking back into the Łódź ghetto and hanged.[12] Lolek went, and we never heard from him again. When Lolek's parents still believed they were leaving Łódź—before Lolek intervened—they sold their extra food. Instead of going off to Poznań or wherever, they died of malnutrition in the ghetto.

---

[11] In 1940 and the first half of 1941, enough healthy men and women volunteered for work outside the ghetto to meet German demands. In November, 1941, the ghetto Bureau of Labor had difficulty filling a German request for one thousand workers and began taking workers by force. Dobroszycki, *The Chronicle*, 46-47, 81-82.

[12] Poznań was in the Warthegau, northeast of Łódź. Dobroszycki, *The Chronicle*, 228, reports that such a hanging took place on July 22, 1942.

After a few weeks with Chaim's family in 1940, I moved again. You see, when my father was taken, I lost a sense of home. When we were evicted from Adolf Hitler Strasse, from my father's apartment, I lost any feeling of belonging. I was nobody's baby. It didn't matter that much who I lived with. This time I moved in with my stepmother. The one exterior wall of her room was cracked and cold air seeped in. On winter mornings, to determine how far below zero the temperature was outside, I would check the thickness of the ice that had formed inside. In that cold room, we were eight: my stepmother; her sister Bronia and a son, six or seven years old; another sister, Hella, her husband, and two sons, aged eight and twenty; and myself. The younger boys went on the children's transport, in 1942.[13] Hella's husband and Bronia both died of tuberculosis in the ghetto. Hella, her older son, and my stepmother were sent to Auschwitz in 1944 and probably gassed immediately. That's how it was in the ghetto. Crowded rooms, not enough to eat, deportations, disease, and death. But I survived, thanks to my father.

Before the war, my father was a respected and well-connected politician, especially in Jewish circles. He belonged to the liberal Folksparty. As chairman of Jewish small business organizations, he once sued *Orendownik*, the most virulently anti-Jewish newspaper in Poland, for libel. The newspaper had published an article accusing a "merchant with sidelocks" of fraud. My father brought the lawsuit on behalf of Jewish merchants, and he won. As a *dozer*, an elected Jewish city councilman, Father sat on the finance committee, which allotted tax money to soup kitchens, orphanages, and homes for the elderly. He served as chairman of an organization that ran two soup kitchens to feed impoverished Jews during the 1930s depression. He also took food and clothing to Jews in the Zbąszyń refugee camp. To this day, I feel bad if I decline a request for charity. It feels like refusing my father.

Indeed, Father was a champion of the poor. He was always more interested in poor people than in the rich and religious. This made him a "patron saint" of the Jewish underworld and the mafia which dominated it. The Jewish mafia in Łódź was not an organization of extortionists and murderers. Mostly, they were small-time criminals. But they looked out for poor Jews. For example, if a man wasn't paying alimony to his ex-wife, they made sure he started paying. One time they beat up some Polish teenagers, curing the young punks of their habit of attacking Jews in the street.

---

[13] In September, 1942, six thousand children were deported to Chelmno for extermination.

Anatol Chari (right) with friend "Lalka" in summer, 1935

Anatol Chari (left) at school camp outside Łódź in summer, ca. 1937

Some of the mafia leaders were active in Father's organizations, and some, like Szaja Bucik, belonged to the praying house which we attended. Bucik means "little shoe," and Szaja Bucik wore a tall shoe to compensate for his club foot. He owned a tavern and probably a brothel or two. He was also a lieutenant in the inner circle of the Jewish mafia. Sometimes, after services, he invited members of the praying house to his tavern for drinks. Father used his political connections to help people like Bucik. For example, at the mafia's request, he got a man called Wowcio Hoyker—"the hunchback"—out of Bereza-Kartuska, a pre-war Polish concentration camp for habitual criminals.

And they did favors for him. When a street pickpocket stole some things from my cousin's purse, Father called Shaja Magnat. His name meant Shaja "The Rich One." He wore gold-rimmed spectacles and owned some apartment buildings. He was second-in-command of the mafia. A few hours later, Shaja came to our apartment with the stolen items. "Councilman Chari, they never would have touched her if they knew she was your niece," he explained apologetically. Another time, two shoplifters robbed Father's dry goods shop. Father caught one and handed him over to the police. The other one wasn't so lucky. Father called Wowcio Hoyker, who found the thief, beat him beyond recognition, and recovered the stolen merchandise.

It wasn't only the underworld. Father had three sisters, and, as their only brother, he felt obligated to take care of them according to tradition. When I was six or seven, his sister Faiga's husband died, leaving her with a son and two daughters. Father helped put her son, Moniek, through university and law school, and found jobs for her daughters, Esther and Helenka. Now and then, Father would take me to one of the offices where he worked, and it pleased me to hear him addressed as Mr. Councilman or Mr. Chairman. We weren't very religious. I had a bar mitzvah, but quickly grew out of any faith I might have had. Today I consider myself a culinary Jew—I like the food. However, we did go to Saturday morning prayer services. If we went to a private home afterwards, Father might be invited to give an invocation or a speech. I don't remember the speeches, but I remember feeling very proud. Father never finished high school, yet enjoyed reciting poetry. He spoke four languages. Yiddish was his first tongue and Russian his second. When he moved to Łódź, he learned German and Polish. He liked to say, "I look like the average Jew." Somebody asked him what the "average Jew" looked like. "Well," he said, "if you see him in bed, he has the crack down the middle of his ass." That was his sense of humor. Average looking, perhaps, but he wore a distinguished fur coat, and he was well known. Some days he walked me home from school, and one time a polite Jewish man tipped his hat to Father and turned to his son, who was about my age. "This is Councilman Chari and his son," he said.

After they passed, Father said to me, "I look forward to the day when people say, 'This is Tolek Chari and his father.'"[14]

Many years later, in 1972, I volunteered for a few months to work as a dentist alongside the Israeli armed forces, treating Bedouins and other Arabs in El Arish in the Sinai desert. During a weekend visit to Tel Aviv, I met a man named Herb Brin, who owned *Heritage*, a Jewish newspaper in southern California. *Heritage* ran an article about me, and, after I returned home to California, Rabbi Haim Asa invited me to address his congregation at the Temple Beth Tikvah in Fullerton. In the temple, the distinguished rabbi honored me with a seat on the Western Wall. That day I thought my father's wish would have been fulfilled. Unfortunately, Father wasn't there to see it. He missed his wish by over thirty years. He missed it because of his influence in Łódź—the Germans killed him right away. But without his influence, I doubt I would ever have been seated at the Western Wall. I doubt I would have made it through the war.

In the ghetto, it was my stepmother who first figured out how to use Father's influence: she spoke to Rumkowski. Like Father, Chaim Rumkowski was on the *Kehillah*, the Jewish city council, before the war. He was responsible for the Jewish orphanages, so he knew Father well, even though they were from different political parties. The story goes that when the Germans invaded Łódź they asked who on the council was "Eldest," meaning had the most seniority. Thinking they meant *oldest*, Rumkowski came forward. The Germans took away the rest of the council, including my father, and made Rumkowski the chairman of the Jewish Council for the ghetto.[15]   First, though, to be sure he knew who was boss, they gave him a

---

[14] Tolek, the diminutive form of Anatolek, is Anatol's Polish nickname. In English, he goes by Tony.

[15] According to Dobroszycki, *The Chronicle*, xliv, n118, the story about the confusion regarding the "Eldest" "can hardly be taken seriously." Rumkowski received his appointment from the German mayor in letters dated October 13 and 14, 1939. He was ordered to disband the *Kehillah* and select a thirty-member *Ältestenrat* (Council of Elders), more commonly called the "Jewish Council." Trunk, *Łódź Ghetto*, 62-63. It is unclear why Rumkowski was selected. Gustavo Corni, *Hitler's Ghettos: Voices from a Beleaguered Society, 1939-1944*, translated by Nicola Iannelli (London: Arnold, 2003), 83. On a single

beating. I'm not sure if that's exactly how it went, but everyone knew that Rumkowski came home beaten up and then was appointed "Eldest of the Jews." In the ghetto, Chairman Rumkowski had a labor office that assigned jobs. The Germans maintained the ghetto as a source of labor for the war effort. The head of the Ghetto Administration, a German businessman named Hans Biebow, took orders from the German command and subcontracted them to Rumkowski, who ran the ghetto as a big labor camp.[16] To survive, to eat, you needed a job, and there weren't enough jobs for everyone. If you had some training—for example, if you were a tailor or shoemaker—you had work for sure, making goods for the German forces. If you had any kind of connection to the ghetto administration, you could arrange a job. If you didn't get a job, you were in trouble. You were considered worthless and were soon shipped out to someplace worse. My stepmother went to Chairman Rumkowski's office, and, because she was Hinda Chari, wife of Councilman Chari, she received a position as a bookkeeper in a food distribution center. She also made sure Rumkowski, who had authority over tens of thousands of people, remembered Tolek Chari. "Consider Piotr's son to be in my charge," he told her. "I will take care of him as if he were my own."[17]

Hinda Chari was a kind woman and always a good mother to me, and now she tricked me. I needed about six months more of classes to graduate from lyceum, which is the final two years at the gymnasium.[18] Rumkowski had started a private gymnasium in the ghetto, but I wasn't all that eager to continue my education.[19] I was a teenager, turning seventeen that June, and didn't want to go to school. My stepmother went to Rumkowski and

---

day in November, the Germans abducted twenty-two of the Elders. They never returned. Dobroszycki, *The Chronicle*, xliii-xlvi.

[16] As head of the *Gettoverwaltung* (Ghetto Administration), Biebow had the title of *Amtsleiter* (Director). Dobroszycki, *The Chronicle*, xli. While some German authorities viewed the ghetto as a temporary situation, useful only for extracting hidden valuables from Jews, Biebow argued that ghetto residents could be a self-sustaining source of labor. The bureaucratic struggle he faced was to keep the ghetto population sufficiently nourished to work, yet producing more value than they consumed, to justify the ghetto's existence. Browning, *The Origins of the Final Solution*, 116-120, 152-158.

[17] Rumkowski became a widower before the war and had no children. Dobroszycki, *The Chronicle*, xlv.

[18] After grade school, a student typically attended four years of gymnasium, took exams, then had two years of lyceum. However, all six years were spent at a school called a gymnasium. After lyceum, a student was ready to attend university.

[19] Rumkowski Gymnasium opened on March 8, 1940. Dobroszycki, *The Chronicle*, 72, n83.

explained that I was embarrassed because I couldn't afford to attend the school. Her husband, the councilman, was gone, after all. I'm not sure if we could have afforded tuition or not—I wasn't exactly in charge of the family treasury—but I think that's what she told him. Anyway, he gave her a letter that said something like, "Please admit Anatol Chari to school with my compliments." When she brought the letter home, having taken the trouble to help me, I could hardly say no. That was the trick. Now I had to go to school.

I went to Rumkowski Gymnasium for six months, finishing lyceum in November, 1940. I took the normal things—history, Latin, German, Polish, math—earning a Matura certificate, the equivalent of one or two years of college in the US today. At the graduation ceremony, Chairman Rumkowski made a speech and said the future of the nation lies in education. He promised to protect the graduates as best he could. And he did. Of the thirty to forty boys and girls in that graduating class, plus the next year's class, only one died in the ghetto and about half survived the war.[20] The survivors include a world-renowned physicist, a concert pianist, and assorted other doctors and psychiatrists. After we graduated, Rumkowski made sure we got good jobs that paid decent wages (in ghetto money), didn't require physical labor, and brought access to extra food.[21] The food was the most important thing. Ghetto conditions were worsening, and the average food rations, distributed by the ghetto administration, were insufficient for basic nutrition. You could only remain healthy and strong if you ate more than the standard allotment.

I was assigned to the gas department. Bałuty had gasworks before the war, and, at first, ghetto residents with a gas meter in their home could use as much gas for cooking as they could afford. Gas for heating was extremely rare in pre-war Poland. People heated their homes with coal-burning stoves. In fact, the only gas heating in the ghetto that I know of was in the electrical department and gas department—they shared a floor—though I'm sure some ghetto elites had it in their apartments. Gas for cooking was a little more common. If your house or apartment didn't have gas, you had to go to one of the public gas kitchens, where they had fifty burners running off a meter. There you could rent a burner by the hour to cook the evening meal—if you

---

[20] Dobroszycki, *The Chronicle*, 122-123, describes "Festivities for Youth" on January 4, 1942, honoring 85 lyceum graduates—probably from the 1940 and 1941 classes.
[21] Ghetto money, known as *Rumkis*, were used primarily for buying food. Dobroszycki, *The Chronicle*, 140-141. Sierakowiak, *The Diary*, 178, called the currency "Chaimkas."

Matura graduation celebration in ghetto, 1940
(Chaim Rumkowski front row middle, Anatol Chari back row second from left)

had something to cook. My friend Lolek C., who graduated with me, was in charge of reading meters, and sometimes I helped him.[22] Lolek and I looked so much alike that even our own families had trouble telling us apart. People bribed Lolek, with food or money, to misread their meter, and sometimes I received bribes intended for him. My main job, though, was running the storeroom for pipes and valves and other things for installation, and that's how I got sick. It was a thirty-minute walk from my stepmother's icy room with the cracked wall to the gas department. It was winter. The only shoes I now owned had wooden soles, which weren't flexible and didn't absorb impact. Also, the snow would stick to the soles. After walking fifty feet, I was three inches taller. I had to stop every few minutes and scrape off the snow. That was no fun. I was wet and cold. Then, around New Year's Day, 1941, I was all day in the unheated storeroom, taking inventory, and caught a severe cold. I became delirious with a high fever and spent two weeks in bed recuperating. When I was healthy, I left my stepmother and moved back into

---

[22] Lolek C. is not cousin Lolek, who was transported out in 1941.

the tiny kitchen with my grandparents. That was more in the center of town, only a ten-minute walk to the gas department.

Even though the storeroom was cold, I had a good job. Like all ghetto workers, gas workers received a midday soup. I was in charge of distributing the daily soup coupons to the other gas department employees. I would write the date on the coupons, which had to be used that day. The ghetto factories, which produced clothing, hats, furniture, knapsacks, metal items, and other things, were called *ressorts*—the German word for workplace—and most *ressort* laborers received their midday soup at work. Large kitchens prepared the soup. Typically, soup kitchens were located inside the *ressorts* they served, though some *ressorts* received their soup in kettles delivered from kitchens located elsewhere. The idea was that you only received lunch if you were at work. But gas workers, because we often roamed throughout the city, could use soup coupons at any soup kitchen. The soup was mostly water, it lacked protein, and one soup would only fill your mouth, not your stomach. It wasn't enough.[23] But I was privileged. Rumkowski was looking out for me. Because of my father—and my stepmother's trick—I got into Rumkowski Gymnasium, then got a good job that brought extra soups. See, nobody was counting carefully, so when I distributed the soup coupons, I kept two or three extra for myself. I could get a bigger lunch, fill my stomach. Maybe I wasn't well nourished, but, unlike other people in the ghetto, I wasn't going hungry. I was riding my father's coattails.

I had other help, too. Before the war, the Kotlicki family lived in the same Piotrkowska apartment building as my family. The Kotlickis had money. They lived in a very nice apartment, in the front of the building, overlooking the street. We lived on one side of the building, neither the richest nor the poorest. The poorest were in the back, farthest from the street. I only met the Kotlickis after the Germans arrived and enforced an evening curfew. To pass the evenings, I played cards in their apartment and got to know Hanka, who was my age or maybe a little younger. She lived with her mother, a sister, and two brothers. Around that time I had a dream. Sitting at their table, I saw someone I didn't recognize walk in carrying a baby. Not long after I had the dream, it came true. I was playing cards at the Kotlickis, and I saw that very scene. It was Hanka's aunt, who I hadn't met,

---

[23] In 1940, German officials decided that ghetto food rationing should be the "nutritional minimum," similar to "prison fare." However, wartime scarcity and anti-Jewish ideology meant ghetto provisioning remained below these minimal standards. Browning, *The Origins of the Final Solution*, 153-158.

carrying one of her two-year-old twin boys. The dream doesn't mean anything, but it wouldn't be the last time I correctly dreamed the future.

Hanka's father was in the textile business—like almost everybody in Łódź—but had already emigrated to Israel. He was trying to arrange to move the whole family, and then the war came. When we were forced into Bałuty, the Kotlicki family acquired a decent second-story apartment—decent by ghetto standards. They had a gas meter, so they could cook food. They had three or four rooms for the five of them plus Hanka's aunt, her small twins, and another guy. The guy went on the work transport with my cousin Lolek in 1941. The twins went on the children's transport in 1942. Hanka's mother and brothers died in the camps after the ghetto was liquidated in 1944. Hanka and her younger sister Uka managed to survive.

In the ghetto, Hanka became my girlfriend. Her aunt got a job supervising a large soup kitchen on the first floor of their apartment building. It produced four to five hundred soups per day for delivery to *ressort* workers. I could eat the midday soup at any *ressort* kitchen in the ghetto, wherever I happened to be, and I always happened to be at this one. Hanka's aunt took care of me. I could use my extra coupons, I got more soup per ticket, and I got thicker soup, with potatoes and vegetables scooped from the bottom of the kettle. Once, when the aunt wasn't there, I got a "normal" soup. I couldn't believe it. This is what people get to eat? I was beginning to realize just how privileged I was. While other's got a mouthful, I filled my stomach. Then I'd go upstairs and fool around with Hanka.

Privilege was important, but you also had to take initiative, even if it was risky. As my father liked to say, "If you don't take any chances, you'll never land in jail." In early 1941, gas and electricity were rationed and, eventually, the Germans ordered the removal of the gas meters.[24] You know, save the gas for the war effort and make ghetto life more miserable. The gas department was permitted to leave twenty-five meters in operation, and the head of the department kept one for himself and one for our office. He also allowed some of his workers to choose one or two meters to leave running. I made sure the Kotlickis could keep theirs. They began using it to run a public kitchen in the front room of their upstairs apartment, with maybe ten or twelve burners for rent by the hour. But it was illegal. It wasn't an official kitchen. The Kotlickis, not Rumkowski's administration, received the rents.

---

[24] Limitations on electricity usage were announced on March 3, 1941. On June 15, 1941, the ghetto administration took control of the gas kitchens. Trunk, *Łódź Ghetto*, 52.

To cover it up, I asked Lolek C. not to read their meter. He just recorded the standard allotment—twenty-five cubic meters or whatever it was, I don't remember exactly—on their bill every month. One day, he and I were both sick, and a substitute went and read their meter—read it correctly. Four hundred cubic meters! The gas department confiscated the meter. But the employee who removed the meter was my subordinate. I was the one who distributed the parts for connections or repairs, and I told him how I wanted this job done. I probably had to bribe him with some food or something. I don't remember. He took out the meter and capped the pipe. A day or two later, he went back and reopened the connection to the burners—without the meter. The Kotlicki kitchen had gas again, as much as they wanted, without cost, for as long as the ghetto existed. They had income, the burners kept their apartment warm, they could cook what was available, and no waiting in line. What more could you ask for? It was like taking a helicopter to work instead of sitting on a crowded freeway. And downstairs, I got a super midday soup and a warm place to eat it.

That's how things worked in the ghetto. If you had the right connections and knew how to use them, you could get a decent job and help yourself and those around you. More and better food. Better living conditions and working conditions. In a place where thousands were dying of malnutrition and disease, such privilege was critical. It helped, too, just knowing you had it better than the next guy. I never felt sorry for myself in the ghetto. You can compare your situation to the better life you left behind, or you can compare yourself to the ones below you. I always knew I had it better than others. Without my connections, I might have been a "4711." That's the name of a German perfume company, and that's what we called the ones who cleaned the outhouses and carried the waste to fields on the ghetto's edge. That was a real bad job. I was a lot better off taking inventory in the cold storeroom in the gas department. Knowing that gave me some comfort. It made me less miserable. It gave me hope. There was definitely a privileged class in the ghetto. Thanks to my father, I was in it.

But I still caught typhoid fever. There was a typhoid epidemic in the ghetto, spread by lice. One day, in 1942, after a visit to the barber, I went home and scrubbed my head with a towel. We rarely took baths in the ghetto. Water wasn't always available. I think there was soap, but it was rationed. Yet I don't recall people smelling bad. Perhaps we got used to it. Anyhow, I scrubbed my head and found a louse on the towel. I can remember lots of bed bugs in the ghetto, but only this one louse. One lousy louse, and I came down ill—can you imagine? Somebody forgot to tell the louse that I was privileged. A doctor quarantined my grandparents in their room and sent me to a hospital.[25] My grandfather tried to cheer me up. "Listen," he said, "typhoid fever—at least you know what you have. You could have caught a cold or pneumonia and God knows what would have happened." Great. I was soon lying in a bed, semi-conscious with high fever, in a hospital ward with twenty or thirty other patients, and my grandparents couldn't leave their little kitchen, but at least I knew what I was dying of.

Aunt Eva, who lived in the room next to my grandparents, saved me. She was an executive secretary in the leather department, which oversaw the leather factories in the ghetto, and she had access to Rumkowski. She went to see him, told him where I was, and he kept his promise. He looked after me as if I was his son. He made sure the doctors knew I was a special patient. They transferred me to a "private room"—four beds, three patients, and all the food you could eat. There were different diets, depending on a patient's condition, but in the "private room" we could choose any of the diets or all of them. We had a sugar jar in the room, so we could sweeten the brown water we called "coffee" or whatever it was they gave us to drink. I received glucose injections that were not available to the general population. Once I got an orange, which was unheard of. It was a "rich" man's life, even for a mostly semi-conscious patient, delirious with high fever. I do remember dreaming that Rumkowski didn't survive the war and that I did. In reality, I was closer to dying, but in my dream I had hope. One morning, I woke from my delirium and discovered a cup of gray water with some fat floating on the surface. When the nurse came in, I told her that someone had left dishwater on my nightstand. "Don't sin," she said. "That's the soup for the 'class three' diet." I really thought it was dishwater. That's how spoiled we were in our "private room." We also had a visitor now and then. A pretty girl named Celinka worked as a nurse's assistant or something. She would come in, sit on the extra bed, and flirt with me. That helped, too.

Finally, I was ready to leave. The staff tried to keep me there, but I didn't feel comfortable staying in the hospital. I just didn't trust the situation. So I checked out. The doctor in charge of my case came running into my room.

---

[25] In 1942, the ghetto had three hospitals with a total of 1,550 beds. The hospital for contagious diseases was located on Drewnowska Street. Dobroszycki, *The Chronicle*, 225-226. Official records note 4,403 cases of typhoid fever during the ghetto's existence. Over half were in 1942. Trunk, *Łódź Ghetto*, 205.

"Who allowed you to go home?" she asked angrily.

"Nobody. I just want to go home."

Selections for extermination began in January, 1942.[26] The Germans took all five thousand Gypsies, who had been isolated in one section of the ghetto. They also removed those Jews not considered useful as workers—the sick, the elderly, and children. Later that year, after I left the hospital, one selection included all the hospital patients. I would have been out of the hospital by then, anyway, even if I hadn't checked myself out.[27] Probably. I'm glad I left.

I was very weak when I left the hospital. Typhoid fever is a very debilitating disease. I could barely walk. There were few telephones in the ghetto, so I couldn't call my grandparents, and there was no public transportation. The Łódź streetcar routes cut through the ghetto, but were fenced off from ghetto residents. The Poles went past on trolleys. The ghetto residents crossed over the tracks on wooden bridges. Somehow, I made it to my grandparents' little house behind the fence and walked in unannounced. Everyone was happy. I was so weak, though, that I believed I wouldn't survive—not as a gas worker, not even with a few extra midday soups. To regain my strength, I needed more food.

I went to see Rumkowski. I climbed the steps of one bridge over the streetcar tracks and was so exhausted I had to rest before crossing. I was in pretty bad shape. I think it was April, 1942. I remember the spring weather. Outside of Rumkowski's office, there was a line of maybe twenty or thirty people waiting to see him. He came out with his secretary—a German Jew named Fuchsówna—and went down the line, asking what people wanted.[28] When he came to me, I said, "Chairman Rumkowski, I'm Piotr Chari's son." When he heard my father's name, he looked up. "I was just in the hospital."

"Yes, I know."

"Sir, I'm awfully tired. I need a job with food so I can get back on my feet."

---

[26] From January through May, 1942, the Germans sent sixty thousand people, including five thousand Roma (Gypsies), from the Łódź ghetto, by train, to be killed in gas vans at Chełmno, thirty-seven miles away. They were told they were being resettled to smaller towns where food was more readily available. In September, sixteen thousand more met the same fate. Trunk, *Łódź Ghetto*, 267.

[27] The hospitals were emptied and the patients removed from the ghetto on September 1, 1942. Dobroszycki, *The Chronicle*, 248-250; Adelson and Lapides, *Łódź Ghetto*, 321-323.

[28] Dora Fuchs headed the Central Secretariat in the ghetto. Dobroszycki, *The Chronicle*, 120 n10. Ghetto residents called her Fuchsówna, which referred to her unmarried status.

"Would you rather work in a kitchen or a bakery?"

"Either one is fine."

Rumkowski turned to his secretary. "Find a job for him."

That's what I wanted. It was more than just "fine." This was a million-dollar lottery ticket. But Rumkowski wasn't finished. He said to me, "You'll hear from me in a couple of weeks. In the meantime, let me give you some extra rations." The secretary gave me special ration cards. I hadn't even asked for that!

Ration cards were different from midday soup coupons. The coupons went to workers each day they worked. Ration cards came out every two weeks, and everybody got one. You took your card to one of the distribution stores, stood in line, and collected your allowance of food. Actually, you purchased the food with the ghetto money you earned at work. The ration card was simply the right to buy a certain amount of food. The salary was usually just enough to buy the rations. We received bread, which we ate for breakfast. Sometimes there was marmalade, sometimes there was a bit of artificial honey made from sugar. It depended on what the Germans had provided for the ghetto that month. Normally, the rations included potatoes or vegetables or barley—things you could cook for dinner. Again, it depended on the Germans. One summer all we ate were pumpkins. Infrequently, there was meat. But a quarter pound of meat per person doesn't exactly last two weeks. As the war went on, the rations got smaller. Meanwhile, the privileged class got special rations. Usually, this was based on your job. In the right position—a factory manager, a ghetto policeman—you received special ration cards for the special distribution stores. More and better food. No waiting in line. That's what Rumkowski's secretary gave me—special ration cards.

That's all she gave me. I went back to work at the gas department and waited. Two weeks went by, my special rations ran out, and I didn't hear from her. I was still very weak. It's a good thing I had a desk job. During a lunch break, I returned to the secretary, and reminded her, "The chairman said I was going to get another job." That was the right thing to do. She sent me to a soup kitchen to be the assistant manager of the storeroom. Sort of like senior helper to the junior janitor. Not a position that brought special rations. But there was food. The kitchen made soup for *ressort* workers, and, officially, the kitchen workers were allowed to eat two soups. But who was counting? The first day I ate ten soups. The second day only seven or eight. Eventually, I settled down to four or five. This meant that, except for my ration of bread, I didn't have to eat at home. Grandfather and I always gave our rations to Grandmother, and she cooked evening meals for the three of us. Since I could now fill up at work, the two of them would have more to eat.

The new job had another perk. The storeroom manager sat upstairs and, as the assistant manager, I would go into the basement to supervise two other guys. They weighed potatoes and vegetables in baskets, then took them upstairs to the kitchen for the soup preparation. It was all supposed to be carefully measured—maybe half a pound of beets or potatoes per soup for maybe four hundred soups a day. Something like that. But nobody would notice if a few potatoes were missing. The two workers explained to me how it would work, and I said okay. There was a small hole in the wall leading to the adjoining basement. They would pass the potatoes through, the janitor next door would collect them, and then the four of us would share what we had organized. That's what we called it. Organizing. *Organizować.* It wasn't stealing. Stealing was *kraść*, when you took from another individual. If you took food from the other guy, he would die. If you took it from the kitchen—from the common pot, so to speak—well, that was the only way to live. That was our code of ethics, circa 1942. You had to organize extra food, take the initiative. You had to look for or create the opportunity to organize extra food. You couldn't survive without it. We couldn't organize much at this kitchen, but every little bit that I took home helped feed Grandmother and Grandfather.

That's how it was for some months in 1942. It was more or less an uneventful period for my grandparents and me in our little room. Others weren't doing so well. See, when the potatoes arrived at the ghetto, they were already half rotten, so the distribution stores gave them out right away. A person would get maybe forty kilos of half-rotten potatoes for the whole winter. They would be gone in three weeks. Then what would you do? The ghetto was starving. The typhoid fever epidemic came and went. Thousands died. Thousands more arrived. In autumn, 1941, the Germans had brought to Łódź twenty thousand Jews from Germany, Czechoslovakia, and elsewhere in central Europe.[29] They were more westernized. Their pre-war standard of living had been higher than in Poland. They arrived well dressed, well fed,

---

[29] Dobroszycki, *The Chronicle*, 93, reports 19,883 newcomers on 21 transports "from Germany, Austria, Luxembourg, and Bohemia" arrived from October 17 to December 13, 1941. In 1942, about 12,000 of these *Reichsjuden* were deported to the Treblinka death camp. Corni, *Hitler's Ghettos*, 182.

and totally unprepared for ghetto life. They didn't have connections in the ghetto administration. They didn't speak the local language. They didn't know how to organize extra food and didn't have the opportunity. We had moved into the ghetto and adapted as conditions gradually worsened. These people came right into a miserable situation. The transition was traumatic. A real shock. They were totally disorganized. They lived in barracks with twenty or so to a room. They weren't assigned work right away, so no midday soup. They had to sell their nice clothes to get food. Many died that winter. The ones who survived eventually got jobs and rooms and integrated into ghetto life. In November, five thousand Gypsies arrived in the ghetto from the Austria-Hungary border region.[30] The Germans incarcerated them in an isolated area, fenced off from the Jewish residents. Nobody had contact with them, except the guys who drove "hearses"—horse-drawn wagons that could carry a few corpses. They were making several trips a day from the Gypsy area to the ghetto cemetery. They said it was pretty bad at the Gypsy camp.[31] The Germans treated Gypsies worse than they treated Jews. The Gypsies were in Łódź for only three weeks, then were transported out and gassed at Chełmno, in January.

As I said earlier, 1942 was a time of transports to extermination camps. The Germans were eliminating those supposedly not useful for the war effort. On selection days, everyone was supposed to line up in the street. Those who tried to hide were shot on sight. The Gestapo came through and pointed out who they wanted.[32] The Jewish police took the condemned to a prison camp in the ghetto, on Krawiecka Street, where they were held until the trains were ready. Aunt Sarah—the one who had taken food to Father in prison—was unhealthy, visibly emaciated, and they took her in the very first selection. I wore my good suit on selection days. I figured that the better I looked, the less likely I would be picked.

So when I say it was an uneventful period, take it with a dose of salt, which also was rationed. With five midday soups, I had enough to eat. With my share of the rations, and a few organized potatoes, my grandparents had about double the average food. They ate a midday soup at the leather *ressort*

---

[30] The Gypsies began arriving on November 5, 1941. Dobroszycki, *The Chronicle*, 82.
[31] From November 12 to December 1, 1941, the ghetto Department of Burial interred 213 corpses from the Gypsy camp. Dobroszycki, *The Chronicle*, 85-86.
[32] In early 1942, Rumkowski's administration drew up a list of deportees. For the September deportations, the Germans made the selections themselves. Corni, *Hitler's Ghettos*, 280-281.

where they worked. Actually, my grandfather was a leatherwork supervisor and instructor, a position with special rations. My grandmother was the instructor's wife. She arrived at the *ressort* around ten in the morning, ate her soup at noon, and gave the appearance of doing something useful. When the Gestapo inspected the factory, she must have fooled them. When the Gestapo transported the elderly to their deaths, my grandparents weren't chosen. They didn't line up in the street for the selection. I went out in my good suit, looking relatively well nourished. They stayed in their little house, invisible from the street, and the Germans never checked there. Had they been found, they would have been shot. In that house, we were organizing electricity for cooking and heating. Most rooms in the ghetto had electricity, but, like food rations, the electricity rations decreased as the war went on. The electricity came through a meter in our room—a limiter—and, with a little know-how, a person could bypass the limiter and keep the electricity flowing freely. One of the Maks next door did this for us. So in our cramped room, the three of us were warm and had enough to eat. As they say, life was "beautiful." For us. Then things got better.

There was competition among the Germans regarding the policing— actually the looting—of the Łódź ghetto. Fear of disease kept the Germans out of the ghetto, so they ran it by proxies. Rumkowski had a Jewish police force, the *Ordnungdienst*. Their tasks included keeping order—no fighting, no break-ins, no stealing building materials for fuel—and guarding the perimeter so that ghetto residents didn't approach the fence and get shot by Germans. Rumkowski's police worked with the Kripo, the German criminal police, who had an office on the edge of the ghetto. The Gestapo had their own ghetto police, the *Sonderkommando*.[33] At first, there were only twenty or thirty of these "Sonders," and they kept a low profile. Their main job was to confiscate valuables from their fellow ghetto residents and hand over the loot to the Gestapo. If Rumkowski's police found valuables, they gave them to the Kripo. You were supposed to surrender any gold, diamonds, jewelry, and foreign money that you brought into the ghetto, and if they thought you were hiding something, the Kripo or Gestapo would try to beat it out of you. They beat one guy who swore up and down that he didn't have anything. He wouldn't talk, so they found his wife, and she told them where the valuables

---

[33] Dobroszycki, *The Chronicle*, 43 n57, says the *Sonderkommando* (Special Unit) of the *Ordnungdienst* (Order Service) was later renamed *Sonderabteilung* (Special Department).

were. Then they killed him. That was the contest—who would get Jewish gold, the Gestapo or Kripo.

Then, in 1942, the Gestapo brought David Gertler back to the ghetto and put him in charge of the Sonders. Gertler was a Łódź Jew who had been working as a stool pigeon for the Gestapo in the Warsaw ghetto. With Gestapo backing, Gertler was on equal footing with Rumkowski, and he enlarged the *Sonderkommando* to three or four hundred policemen. The new Sonders would be in charge of guarding the food storage and distribution, something Rumkowski's police never did. Maybe the Gestapo wanted to end the corruption, inefficiency, and all the organizing in the ghetto operation. Maybe it was just greed. As for Gertler, let's just say he was well nourished...to an excess. There was a joke about that in the ghetto. In 1943, Gertler disappeared, apparently removed by the Germans.[34] Once or twice, the privileged rations included a can of meat—beef, or something close to it, maybe horse, for the privileged population, and pork for the super privileged. The joke was that now we know what happened to Gertler: someone recognized him in a can of pork.

There's another story I heard about Gertler. After the ghetto was sealed, in 1940, he arranged for thirty to forty rich Jews to move from Łódź to Warsaw under the protection of the Gestapo.[35] They were told to bring all their valuables. At that time, mail still went between the two ghettos, but they never wrote from Warsaw to anyone in Łódź. They were never heard from again. This was well-known. In the 1970s, another survivor told me that he had seen their corpses delivered to the Marysin cemetery the day after they departed. He suggested that the reason Gertler refused to testify against his Gestapo handler, a guy named Schmidt, is he didn't want his complicity in these killing revealed. I don't know if it's true or not. It's hearsay. There were lots of rumors in the ghetto. And afterward.

---

[34] Gertler was arrested by the Gestapo on July 12, 1943. His disappearance was the subject of much speculation in the ghetto. Dobroszycki, *The Chronicle*, 43 n57, and 359.
[35] Dobroszycki, *The Chronicle*, 55 n65, confirms that before 1943 a few ghetto residents received permission to go to Warsaw, but "at horrendous cost—gold, diamonds, and foreign currency were often used for payment." For example, "On January 19, [1942] 27 residents of the ghetto left for Warsaw with special permission." On March 25, 120 more went, and another 160 on June 3. Dobroszycki, 123, 136, 197. Sierakowiak, *The Diary*, 158, mentions a busload to Warsaw on April 22, 1942. According to Oskar Rosenfeld, *In the Beginning was the Ghetto: Notes from Łódź*, translated by Brigitte Goldstein (Evanston, IL: Northwestern University Press, 2002), 197, "It was [Gertler] who, presumably, against payment of 1,000 to 2,000 marks, officially took Jews from the ghetto in big trucks to Warsaw and make money that way."

That's not the point. The point is I became a Sonder. Rumkowski was still looking out for his graduates. In 1941, a second class had finished lyceum at Rumkowski Gymnasium, but then the Germans shut down all schools in the ghetto.[36] The classroom space was needed to house the new arrivals from outside Poland. Rumkowski wanted to protect the few educated ones for the future, and the new jobs in the expanded *Sonderkommando* were obviously privileged positions. They would have more to eat and be safe from deportation. Rumkowski had all the male graduates meet with him in an administration office across the street from a big church on a square called Plac Kościelny.[37] A few female graduates worked in his *Ordnungdienst*, but only men were wanted for the Sonders. He interviewed us, one by one, and asked if we wanted to become policemen. Everyone said yes. Everyone except me. I was pretty happy working in the kitchen, eating lots of soup. I didn't care to change jobs. You have to understand, I was a teenager, imprisoned in a ghetto, during a war. I wasn't exactly planning a career. I just wanted enough to eat. I went to see my stepmother, who worked at a food distribution store nearby, and told her about my decision. It was okay with her. But her co-workers didn't agree. "It's going to be the best job in the ghetto," they kept telling her, "an important job, a prestigious position." They said I was stupid and irresponsible. They really got on me. "Go back," they insisted. "Go back and tell the chairman you want to get in." I went back, and Rumkowski was gone. He was walking down the street with his entourage, with a couple of his policemen around him. I chased after them.

"Mr. Chairman, I'm Tolek Chari."

"I know who you are. What do you want?"

"Mr. Chairman, I changed my mind. I'd like to join the new police force."

"Fine. Come tomorrow to the Sonder office and we'll get you in."

That's how it happened. I became a Sonder. Because of Rumkowski. Because of my father.

---

[36] The schools were closed on September 26, 1941. Sierakowiak, *The Diary*, 133.

[37] According to Dobroszycki, *The Chronicle*, 270, on October 11, 1942, "The Chairman summoned the young men who had obtained their gymnasium degrees in the ghetto to the Personnel Department and hired those who were physically fit on the spot." Sierakowiak, *The Diary*, 232, reported, on November 24, 1943, "New people are still being accepted for the Sonderabteilung."

2

A SONDER'S LIFE

I was a policeman from autumn, 1942, when the *Sonderkommando* force was enlarged, until late summer, 1944, when the Łódź ghetto was liquidated. There were several hundred Sonders working for Gertler. It was definitely a privileged position. Unlike the regular ghetto police—Rumkowski's *Ordnungdienst*—who wore armbands, we had full uniforms.[38] Wearing the uniform gave you a sense of authority and prestige. In a ghetto filled with nobodies, you were somebody. We walked into stores that were off-limits to the general population. We received special rations cards, which meant larger rations, better quality food, and no standing in a long line at the general distribution store. My grandparents and I would get enough to eat. Sonders didn't have to worry about being deported—at least not at first—and we didn't have to perform difficult physical labor. We watched others do the physical labor. We were the food police, with lots of opportunities to organize extra food. This wasn't a dog guarding the apples. This was a dog guarding the meat! We worked two weeks on a day shift, then one week on a night shift, but every day you had a different job—for two reasons. First, the ghetto administration usually didn't know in advance when a food shipment would arrive and require police supervision, so the assignments had to be flexible. Second, if a policeman knew his job in advance, or had the same duty for several days running, he could plan ways to organize food, maybe with outside help. With daily shuffling, it was harder to plan in advance.

---

[38] The regular police wore "distinctive caps, blue and white armbands with Stars of David, and carried rubber nightsticks." Dobroszycki, *The Chronicle*, 3 n3.

My first assignment was night duty in Marysin, the district on the edge of the ghetto where the trains arrived. Potatoes and vegetables arrived at the train station, then were taken by horse and wagon to an open area where they typically were stored for a few days before distribution. My job that first night was being a traffic cop at the storage area where the wagons arrived. In Yiddish, the wagon drivers were called *balagulas*. They were tough guys, with little education and less respect for the law. Before the war, they were connected to the Jewish mafia and underworld. In 1940, when the ghetto first began, the Gestapo put a number of butchers, bakers, and *balagulas*— three b's—on a transport, probably to a work camp. I suspect that Rumkowski thought the three b's would be difficult to control and wanted them out. Now, on my first Sonder duty, I had to oversee *balagulas* at work. The first driver arrived, and, politely, I directed him where to unload the produce. The big man looked at me and said, dismissively, "Look who's going to give me orders." That was my initiation. A policeman has to project authority. I learned quickly. On-the-job training. When the second driver pulled up, I took a different approach. As we say in Polish, *rostawić rodźine po kątach*—I put his family in the proper corner. In English, something like, "Listen, you sonofabitch, put the potatoes over there." That got his attention. That night I also became a Yiddish speaker. In my father's house, we spoke Polish. That's what educated Jews spoke in Łódź, to separate themselves from the Jewish working class. My grandparents spoke Yiddish at home, and I answered them in Polish. When I did say something in Yiddish, Grandmother complained about my Polish accent. As a policeman, though, I had to communicate with the uneducated ghetto workers, so I learned Yiddish, and fast.

Along with the potatoes and vegetables, the trains brought sacks of sugar. A Sonder had to supervise the men unloading the sacks so they wouldn't organize any sugar. They weren't allowed to open any sacks, but they always managed to drop a sack so that it broke. It was okay for the workers—and the policeman on duty—to take sugar from the broken sack and sweeten their "coffee." The "coffee" was of undetermined origin. Maybe it was from burnt apples. Maybe it was from grain. Substitute coffee. When the sack broke, we didn't add sugar to our substitute coffee, we added substitute coffee to our sugar. We dipped our cups into the sugar, then, to disguise it, poured a little brown liquid on top. It looked like substitute coffee, but was more like syrup. We needed the calories. Any food was good for you. That's what it was like as a Sonder. You were around food. There were opportunities. Not that you could lay your hands on everything all the time. But you could get some things some of the time. It was better than being one of Rumkowski's police, guarding the perimeter. There was no food in watching the fence.

As a policeman, you didn't need to write daily activity reports about everything you did, but you were required to write a report for "crimes" and other improper things. At night, the ghetto was kept dark, supposedly so that Allied aerial bombers wouldn't target Łódź. I would write in my report if light was coming out a window, or if a door wouldn't close, things like that. I didn't write things that got people into real trouble, and nobody ever questioned my reports. I never turned in anyone for organizing food. For example, Sonders on duty in the bakeries had to count the loaves of bread baking in the wood-burning ovens. These were large loaves, over four pounds each. You counted as they went in and as they came out. The workers would sneak a few extra loaves into the oven. When they took out the extra loaves, they would try to distract you. Someone might say, "Mr. Sonder, can you check me? I need to go to the toilet." The policeman was supposed to frisk the worker so he wouldn't carry out bread or flour. One time I said, "No, not now." Unable to distract me, they didn't dare to remove two extra loaves they had baked. Later, the two loaves came out all burned up. I didn't report that.

There were lots of techniques for organizing food. If your job gave you access to potatoes or vegetables, you could smuggle them home in your clothes. You would tie your pants legs tight at the ankles or your sleeves tight at the wrists and the food wouldn't drop out. We called them "arm potatoes." In the bakeries, where the loaves were carefully counted, workers had to fix the books when they organized bread. They would declare that mice had eaten some bread or it had become moldy. They were supposed to rework the moldy bread into the fresh bread, but they could get away with sneaking out a loaf or two. Soup was harder to organize. You couldn't pour it down your pants leg. It helped to know the woman who ladled your soup, as she could give you the watery soup from the top or scoop down deep and give you pieces of potato and vegetables. Any little bit of nutrition helped. I'm sure there were other ways to organize extra food. This wasn't a secret business. Everyone knew it was going on. Everyone knew it was necessary. The food rations received by the general population were not enough to live on. Some people in the ghetto looked emaciated. We called it *klepsydra*,

Jewish ghetto police, the Sonderkommando, Łódź, 1943 (Anatol Chari far left)

meaning their time was running out.[39] If you weren't *klepsydra*, you were obviously organizing food. As a Sonder, I was supposed to prevent food organizing, but I was deeply involved in it, and when others did it, I looked the other way.

Once, I was on duty in Marysin, guarding the vegetable storage area, and a Sonder *szef*, or lieutenant, showed up for inspection.[40] There were five or six of these lieutenants, and two always worked in the Sonder office. The others roamed the city, showing up unannounced to see where we were and what we were doing, mostly to remind us that we were under supervision. While this lieutenant was present, one of the cart-pushers who delivered potatoes to the soup kitchens was ready to leave, and I had to search him. I patted him down, and he had potatoes hidden all over. Arm potatoes. Leg potatoes. He dared to smuggle out potatoes, even with the police inspector standing right there, because he knew I wouldn't say anything.

Word spread pretty quickly in the ghetto regarding who you could work with and who was a snitch. Most people wouldn't snitch. The guys in the kitchen basement where I used to work—the ones who organized potatoes

---

[39] *Klepsydra*, literally "water thief," was the ancient Greek term for a water clock used to track the time allotted to a speaker in an Athenian court.

[40] *Szef* is Polish for "chief," but in this context is better understood as a police lieutenant.

through the hole in the wall—they got caught. I was afraid they would say I had been involved, but they didn't talk. Several butchers knew they could work with me, but they were still careful. When I was on duty in their meat distribution store, they would say, "Mr. Sonder, I think we have more meat here than we need," or something like "I think they miscounted and gave us two extra sausages." Translation: We can organize a little bit from the common pot. They were supposed to send extra meat back to the central distribution store, so they would ask me, "Shall we return it?" Translation: Do you mind if we organize?—we'll give you a share. I would respond, "We'll see what's left at the end of the day." Translation: Okay, I'm in. They knew me well in two meat stores, and word got around. If I was on duty at a different meat store, and one of my butcher friends came to collect his ration, he would wink at the butcher in the store, letting him know I was alright.

Meat was a very valuable item in the ghetto because nobody was getting enough protein, and it became scarcer as the war went on. While supervising the delivery of canned meat one night, I put three or four cans under my jacket, then hid them in the bushes for retrieval the next day. When we delivered the load, we were four cans short. I said, "They must have fallen off the truck. I didn't see it." End of story. That was small stuff. Shaja Magnat, my father's friend from the mafia leadership, managed to organize some leather. A whole railway car full of leather! The Kripo beat him, but he wouldn't say where he had hidden it. They beat him to death. After the war, when the ghetto was demolished, the leather was found.

My biggest organizing coup took place in a bakery on Rybna Street. We were on duty in pairs, one Sonder to keep an eye on the other. My partner was a dumb sonofabitch. He was either a German or a Czech Jew, but he definitely had the discipline of a German. He was proper. He followed the rules. You couldn't organize with him around. His attitude was, "I won't eat, and neither will anybody else." On this day, we were supervising the delivery of flour. He stood in the street, watching the delivery cart and the front door. I stood in the front hallway of the building, from where I could see the door leading to the first-floor bakery and, on the opposite side of the hallway, a stairway to the higher floors. Between the two of us, we could observe the workers carrying sacks of flour from the cart to the bakery. But we couldn't see each other. The workers knew my attitude, knew I would cooperate with them. They were what we called *biała gwardja*—the White Guard—the guys who loaded and unloaded heavy sacks, one hundred kilos or whatever.[41] Strong guys. One of them lived on the second floor above the bakery. I let them take a whole sack upstairs and hide it in his room. A whole sack, and the sacks were being counted in the bakery. The White Guard were supposed to dump four sacks right into the container for making bread. They dumped in only three. "Don't worry," they told me, "once the flour is in and mixed up, we can straighten things out." I don't know how they did it. Perhaps they added recycled flour from bread that had spoiled. There's no way you could get away with a whole sack of flour from one mixing, but we did. I got my share and exchanged it for potatoes or bread or maybe some money. Either way, Grandmother had enough food for a long time. My duty partner that day, the dumb sonofabitch, never knew.

The one time I got in trouble for organized food, I wasn't involved. I was on night duty in a bakery, and a lieutenant caught me taking a nap. The bakery workers were loading a cart with bread to deliver to a distribution store, and, in the morning, when the next shift came on, we were two loaves short. I don't know how it happened. Things would disappear in the blink of an eye, nap or no nap. But I got written up for that, and was assigned to two or three weeks on internal duty, which was called *luftschutz* or *luftward*.[42] That meant delivering letters or standing around in the Sonder station all day, holding the door open for Gestapo men. At night, it meant watching for Allied bombers that never came.

Around this time, I was called in to see Gertler. Remember, he was the Sonder head who worked with the Gestapo. Gertler's advisors had drawn up a list of forty Sonders, including me. They had, I think, decided to downsize the force for the sake of discipline, and Gertler, maintaining the appearance of final authority, would choose twenty-five from the list to be fired.[43] While I was waiting to see Gertler, a Sonder sergeant named Singer suggested, "Chari, if you can, try to remind him of your father. It can't hurt." Singer understood that anybody who was somebody in the ghetto knew my father before the war. Gertler had been some sort of insignificant aide, like a courier, in one of Father's organizations. Gertler called me in and interviewed me. How old are you? Who are you with in the ghetto? I think

---

[41] 100 kilos equals 220 pounds.

[42] Literally, air-protection or air-watch.

[43] Dobroszycki, *The Chronicle*, 296, reports "The Order Service was again reduced" in early December, 1942. This reduction probably does not refer to Sonders, although *The Chronicle*, 320, calls a Sonder a "An Order Service man in the Special Department."

he was trying to determine who on the list faced the most hardship and couldn't afford to lose the Sonder position. He wasn't totally heartless. I told him, "I'm Anatol Chari. I'm alone. My father was on the *Beirat* and taken away." He looked up, surprised. The *Beirat* was the advisory board of the Jewish city council in Łódź.

"Piotr Chari?"

"Yes, sir."

I found out later that Gertler's advisors had already put me on the list of twenty-five to be fired, but I guess Gertler took Piotr Chari's son off the list. I didn't lose my job. No one bothered me again. People were aware that both Gertler and Rumkowski knew my father. I had *protekcja*—someone was protecting me. My father's coattails. I never had any more difficulty in the ghetto.

This was in 1943, the year I turned twenty, and my hormones were playing havoc with me. I was having two nocturnal emissions a night. I was no longer spending time with Hanka. There were no movie theatres or automobiles where you could fool around with girls, and I was sleeping in a tiny room with my grandparents. I wanted a place of my own. I had been a Sonder for two or three months, and one day, when I was on duty at the storage area in Marysin, Gertler showed up for inspection. Talk about taking some initiative—I went up to Gertler, reminded him that I was Piotr Chari's son, and asked if I could possibly get my own place so I wouldn't have to live with my grandparents. He told me his office would take care of it. Sure enough, in a week or so, the Sonder office had a letter for me, an open letter from Gertler to the housing department. The lieutenant who gave me the letter asked, "Why didn't you go through the normal channels? You could have applied through us." It wasn't an innocent comment. I had skipped over the lieutenants in the chain of command, and they didn't appreciate this disregard. But I wasn't going to be pushed around now. I felt secure in my protected situation. I replied politely but dismissively, "I know, but I wanted it to get done."

I took the letter to the housing office. The clerk behind the desk gave me three addresses to look at. I found them all unacceptable, uninhabitable, even by ghetto standards. They were small and dark. One for sure, I remember, had a slanted ceiling. You could barely stand up. I went back to the housing office and told the clerk what I thought. She didn't care.

She said, "Too bad. That's all we have."

I said, "Too bad. I'll have to go back to Gertler and tell him you can't fulfill his request."

In Germany, they say there are two types of people, those standing in front of the desks and those sitting behind them. The clerk thought she was behind the desk and I was in front, but I had just put her in front of the desk and Gertler behind it. This changed her attitude.

"Well, there is one more you could look at."

For the rest of my time in the ghetto, I lived at that "one more." It was on the fourth floor of a four-story building, not far from where Grandfather and I collected our special rations. The room was long and narrow, large enough for two beds and a table. There was a wood-burning stove which I probably never used. On one end of the room was the door, on the other a window. The fourth floor had its own water faucet—running water—a big deal in the ghetto. I didn't have to go outside and use the pump. The room had electricity, but there was a limiting device. I could only draw enough power for a light bulb. My friend Maniek R. worked in the electrical department. I knew him from Schweitzer Gymnasium before the war—he was three years behind me—and now he lived across the street from my room. He fixed the wires so that they bypassed the limiter and I could draw enough power for a heating element. I could heat my room. There was one problem. Whenever I connected the heater, all the lights on the entire block would dim. Every couple of weeks, the fuses would blow, and Maniek would have to fix them. Eventually, I got caught, probably on a routine inspection. I came home one morning from night duty, and I had no electricity. I went straight to the electrical department. It was in the same building, on the same floor, as the gas department where I first worked. The people there, including the department head, Diplom Engineer Weinberg, knew me, or at least recognized me as a gas worker. By ghetto standards, Weinberg was a super-privileged man. Before the war, he had been a senior engineer in the Łódź electrical plant. The plans for the Łódź grid were all in his head. They didn't exist on paper. The Germans constantly needed his help to keep the city running. This gave him privilege and influence in the ghetto. He ran the electricity, and, because of his German connections, didn't have to pay much attention to the Jewish administration. He could get food. He had a beautiful apartment on the same floor as the gas and electrical departments. When I found Weinberg at work, he told me they had discovered my ruse. "We have to cut your electricity," he said. "That's the minimum we should do."

"Sir, I'm sorry. It was stupid of me. I promise it won't happen again."

"Alright. We'll turn it back on in a week."

"A week? I'm on night duty. I come home and I can't even heat some water. I need your help now." He sent a worker home with me. The guy's name was Leib. I told him, "My uncle used to deal with an electrical supply house called Brothers Leib on Piłsudki Street".

"Yeah, that was our family business. What's your uncle's name?"

"Tadek." He was married to my mother's sister, Irene.

"Sure," he told me, "I knew him well." Leib and I had common ground. That's a connection. I found that connection so I could arrange for another connection. A reconnection.

"Listen," I asked, "what would it cost to fix my electricity so I won't get caught anymore?" We worked something out. Probably a loaf of bread. He reconnected my electricity around the limiter so that the rest of the block wasn't effected, and I never got caught again. I was organizing all the electricity that I wanted for my room until the last day.

Best of all, it was a room of my own. I could have girls there. When I was on day duty, I could host get-togethers at night. My room became a place where the privileged kids could gather. People like me. Guys with connections. Sonders, bakery managers, not factory workers. The girls were the sisters or daughters of this kind of aristocracy. They were beautiful, beautifully dressed, and well fed. You could tell they were privileged when you saw them in the street. One of them—I don't remember her name—was married to a Kripo stool pigeon, which put her in the privileged class. We hated stool pigeons with contempt, not with respect, but she was very nice, very pretty, and very lonely. The Germans had taken away her husband. So she played cards with us. We sat on the beds in the dark, maybe three guys and five girls. The only entertainment in the ghetto was each other's company. There was no liquor available, but Sonders received a ration of cigarettes—a big deal in the ghetto—and, when we heard the tobacco distribution store had extra cigarettes to sell, we could go buy even more. A Sonder who had worked in a drug store before the war told me that no one bought these lousy cigarettes, made of cheap tobacco or herbs or whatever, until the war began. Now, in the ghetto, they were only for the privileged. At our little parties, we smoked, told jokes, fooled around. Nothing serious. Above the waist only. At two or three in the morning, another Sonder and I would walk everybody home, as it was after curfew. Then I would go to work at seven. The building janitor asked me, "Mister Sonder, don't you ever go to sleep?" One morning, I slept late, slept right through my wind-up alarm clock. I was an hour late for duty, and the sergeant wrote me up. A lower-ranked Sonder, like a corporal, asked, "Chari, what happened?" I explained that I'd been up all night playing poker for ghetto money. I told him who my playing partners were. In our privileged class, everybody knew each other. The corporal relayed my story to the sergeant, and the sergeant tore up his report. "If you had told me what had happened," he said to me, "I never would have written you up." That's how it worked in the privileged class.

When I was on night duty, there were no get-togethers. I came home early in the morning, and all I wanted to do was sleep all day. I was tired, weak, and hungry. No matter how much soup and bread you ate, you didn't get enough protein and you always felt hungry. You could survive, but it wasn't comfortable. If you were asleep, though, you didn't suffer hunger—until you woke up again. And, remember, I was eating much more than the average person in the ghetto. The average man in the ghetto was impotent. It happened to me when I was assigned to internal duty at the Sonder headquarters for several weeks. This meant less access to food—no organizing—though with special rations I still had twice the average diet. Nineteen years old, twice the average diet, and I became impotent—until I got back to organizing more food. So you can imagine that there weren't many men in the ghetto who could perform. A healthy man was a rare thing. Once I was supervising a group unloading potatoes from the train. I had to search the workers if they wanted to go to the outhouse. One girl had me search her every half hour. Finally, I caught on. She was having great fun with this game. Probably a substitute for the real thing. A well-fed policeman, like me, was in demand.

I didn't have sex with the privileged girls, like the stool pigeon's wife, who came to my get-togethers. Perhaps I was too bashful to try. Girls outside the privileged class were a different story. I was on duty in a soup kitchen, watching a girl dish the soup out of a barrel. When the other workers came to dump more soup into her barrel, she backed out of the way, backed right into me. I grabbed her ass. She turned and smiled. I told her where I lived, and I lost my virginity that evening. Her name was Tola. She was from Brzeziny, a small town outside of Łódź known for its tailor shops. We would say, in Yiddish, of their clothes, "*Tandetnie gemacht, trent sich schnell*"—"It's cheaply put together. It tears easily." *Trenen*, the Yiddish word for "tearing," also means "screwing."

Tola and I had an on-going affair, but there were others. Sex was pretty easy with the lower-class girls, even though we didn't invite them to our parties. They were looking for us—able, young men—and they found us, in uniform, on duty. If we were outside in the freezing cold, watching the storage fields in Marysin—well, that wasn't real conducive to fooling around. There was more action with the girls in the warm bakeries. In one bakery, there was a factory girl on temporary reassignment as a bookkeeper. It was a three-month, rotating assignment to allow a factory worker to recoup a little bit. That night, she was recouping with my duty partner, an older policeman more versed in such things than I was. They were on the table, and I was sleeping on a wooden bench. When they finished, she came over to my bench and said, "Let me lie down with you. I'm uncomfortable on the table." Just like that. Another night, another bakery, I was sleeping alone on a narrow bench in the office, and another girl came in to keep me company. She, too, wanted to screw. It wasn't my doing. She wasn't getting any special favors from me. No extra food. No protection. She didn't even know my name. In the ghetto, if you had the chance, you did it, because there might not be a second chance.

I was on duty one morning, checking ID cards at the bridge over the streetcar tracks, the bridge I could barely cross after I came out of the hospital. During the day, everyone was supposed to be at work, so if you were crossing the bridge you had better be an office messenger, a gas worker, an off-duty policeman—someone with a reason to be out roaming—not a *ressort* worker. I stopped a girl, a German Jew, and took her ID. She was supposed to be at her factory job, and now she had a problem. Her ID card was her soup card. She would probably miss the midday soup that day and for sure the next day when she went to the police headquarters to reclaim her card. She said, "Don't turn it in. Tell me where you live, and I'll come pick it up tonight." Thinking back on it, I don't know if she was trying to bribe me with the promise of sex to avoid losing tomorrow's soup, or if she simply wanted sex. The girls from Germany and Czechoslovakia, more westernized countries, tended to be more willing than the girls from Łódź. I sent her back to work and turned in her card. Maybe that was the wrong thing to do—she didn't get any sex *and* she lost the next day's soup. But I wasn't interested in trading police favors for sex. There were enough eager girls in the bakeries. Maybe it was their last gasp, thinking they didn't have much future. I don't know. There was little to lose. We didn't have AIDs or other venereal diseases. Anyhow, it didn't seem frivolous. It wasn't bad. It was mutual consent—their needs and our ability to satisfy them. That's why they would lie down with policemen on the bakery tables. Their hormones didn't go to sleep because of the war. At one point, we received an order: please refrain from using the tables at night because they do have other uses during the day. Use the benches instead.

We were young guys, having a good time, and we bragged about our conquests. Lots of people bragged. I remember seeing a well-built woman, who worked in a large food storage area in the middle of town, stand in the doorway and proclaim, *"Całe ghetto je banie—ja też"*—"The whole ghetto eats pumpkins—me too." It was a play on words. In Polish, "to eat pumpkins" also means "to screw." I'm sure she ate pumpkins with a few Sonders the next time she had night duty. The Don Juans of the ghetto were a prominent Sonder named Sergeant G. and my friend Lutek, a baker. Sergeant G. and I were on duty in Lutek's bakery, and those two guys sat at a table boasting about their conquests. One would say, "I had this girl who was...." He would describe her, and the other would guess who it was. So it went through the night. Lutek even claimed he deflowered a woman whose husband, a fireman, couldn't do the job. I couldn't compete with them. They screwed every woman in sight.

There was a pretty girl, about twenty-four or twenty-five, who was new to the bakery. I don't remember her name, but I remember her wit. She told me that when she saw Gertler with a cracked lip, she remarked, "Gee, you must have had a beginner for a partner." In fact, it was Gertler who arranged the bakery job for her, so I assume she slept with him. Guys were talking about her—she was real friendly—but she never had night duty. I met her on day duty. She was taking a pot of substitute coffee from the oven, and when she backed up, I put my arm around her so she wouldn't fall. My hand touched her breast. Grabbed it, actually. Strictly on accident. She smiled at me, and I thought, "Gosh, if only I had a night or two with her." Wouldn't you know it, I was the first one to have night duty with her. Wouldn't you know it, she was hard to catch. All night I was trying to flirt with her. The following evening, I arrived at the headquarters for my next assignment, and some other guys were heading to her bakery.

"Chari, how was it with her last night?"

"Perfect."

Later, they said it was perfect for them as well. She was getting a reputation. Everybody had just a wonderful time with her. Or so they said. That included Berek K., or Beryl, a fellow policeman who organized even more food than I did.[44] We had enough dirt on each other to have mutual respect. We had to keep each other's secrets—the other knew too much.

He confided in me, "Tolek, I couldn't even touch her. She wouldn't let me."

"Beryl, neither could I." Nobody touched her, but, like they say, a bad reputation is better than none. She eventually married a fireman in the ghetto. I remember Beryl's last name, but I'm not comfortable giving last names of those involved in organizing. I don't want to speak badly of the dead.

During that "perfect" night, I got caught sleeping again. You weren't supposed to sleep in the bakery, of course, but usually there were two of us on night duty, and one could nap while the other kept an eye out. I got so accustomed to sleeping on wooden benches that I could tell the difference between lying on softwood and lying on hardwood. Anyhow, I put so much energy into flirting with the untouchable girl that I laid down and fell asleep around two in the morning. When the inspector, a lieutenant named Rothschild, walked in, I tried to gather myself. I stood up and pulled on my jacket and pretended to be wide awake.

The jacket is another story. I bought it from a Czech who arrived in late 1941, one of those disoriented and unemployed foreign Jews who had to trade their nice clothes for food to survive the ghetto winter. It was a decent gray jacket, but too thin to keep me warm on cold nights. When you were assigned outdoor night duty in the winter, you were temporarily issued a very heavy Sonder overcoat to protect you in sub-zero conditions. When the next Sonder came on duty, you gave it to him. I wanted something warmer of my own to wear over my regular uniform, and I had an idea. When my father was arrested, he was wearing his short fur coat. It disappeared with him. His long fur coat, the one for winter, he left in his closet, and my stepmother brought it to the ghetto and kept it hidden. You couldn't wear a fur coat. The Germans had demanded all our furs, and if you were caught with one, you would be shot for "sabotage"—impeding the war effort.[45] My idea was to use the long fur coat to insulate the gray jacket. My stepmother objected. She was totally devoted to Father. She was saving the coat, she said, for his return. Some people remained naïve longer than others. I'm sure she went to

---

[44] Beryl is the diminutive of Berek.
[45] The compulsory sale of furs, at below market price, was announced by Chairman Rumkowski on December 17, 1940. Dobroszycki, *The Chronicle*, 6-7.

the Auschwitz gas chamber worrying, "How will Piotr Chari find me here? He won't know what happened to me." Finally, I argued that Father's son was more important than Father's coat. Father's son didn't want to get pneumonia. She relented, and I paid a tailor to cut up the fur coat and use it to line the gray jacket. That way, the jacket would be much warmer, and no one could see I was wearing fur.

When the lieutenant caught me sleeping, and I pulled on the jacket and stood up, I didn't fool him. I was half asleep and the jacket was inside out. The fur was showing! Of course, he didn't care about the fur. That was a German concern. He wasn't going to denounce a fellow Sonder and get him killed. But he did write me up for sleeping on duty. Time to use my connections. The lieutenant had a relative who worked as a butcher in the main distribution center for meat. My uncle Arek knew the butcher and sent me to talk to him. The butcher wanted some leather goods, Uncle Arek worked in a leather *ressort*, and we arranged a deal. In exchange for the leather, the butcher convinced the lieutenant, his relative, to tear up the report, and I paid a metalworker to make a real nice silver ring for the lieutenant. As we say, one hand washes the other.

A different lieutenant came to me at work one day and asked for the key to my room. I told him, "You know I'm not hiding anything there." That was true. Since I didn't cook, any food that I organized went straight to Grandmother. "No," he explained, "I need a place to go with my girlfriend." If I remember correctly, he had a girlfriend whose husband was a dentist. The lieutenant and his girlfriend perished during the war. The lieutenant's wife and the dentist got married after the war. Really.

That reminds me of the double whammy. One night, Tola was at my place, and we were doing what we did, and then I walked her home. It was about two in the morning. I still wasn't satisfied, so I knocked on Celinka's door. She was the girl I flirted with in the hospital. She let me in, and, when she understood my intentions, said, "Not here. We'll go to your place." Back in my room, she said, "As long as you dragged me out of bed, you are not going to sleep tonight." That was the wildest night of my young life. There was no sleeping. However, that wasn't the double whammy.

The next morning I was assigned to a large flat-bed wagon drawn by horses and loaded with potatoes. An empty wagon approached from the opposite direction, and that driver knew me. We had done some organizing together. He winked, letting my driver know he could work with me. My driver asked, "Would it be okay, Mr. Sonder, if we took a few potatoes?"

Where it pivoted, the wagon had two horizontal wheels. Inside this turning mechanism, between the wheels, was a space with the bottom closed—perfect for hiding a few potatoes. Like forty kilos' worth. We stopped and filled it up. We were taking potatoes from the distribution center to a soup kitchen. At the distribution center, they had loaded the potatoes into a big pile on the flatbed, then weighed it. When we reached the kitchen, the workers unloaded the potatoes with large baskets. We drove away with our stash, hoping the kitchen manager wouldn't bother with weighing our delivery. The guys with the wagon asked how I wanted my cut. That was the normal practice. I could take my share of the potatoes, or I could give the workers my share in exchange for flour or bread or ghetto money. I usually took some flour for Grandmother and some bread to eat in my room. That was the double whammy—all night with Celinka and my share of forty kilos of potatoes the next day.

Two or three days later, one of the drivers told me, "Listen, Mr. Sonder, the police investigators are going to call you in. Don't worry—it's fixed." Fortunately, those guys knew what they were doing, because I had no idea what was going on. I didn't know the kitchen manager had weighed the potatoes. In the interrogation, the police inspector asked how it could be that my wagon was missing forty kilos. I was ready for this. I had an explanation. At the distribution center, I pointed out, they loaded with shovels, and the dirt goes with the potatoes. At the kitchen, they unloaded with pitchforks, and the dirt falls off. The kitchen manager weighed the baskets filled with potatoes, I suggested, but he didn't weigh the dirt. Well, that wasn't a convincing story. There might be two kilos of dirt, but not forty. The inspector needed a better explanation. Fortunately, *he* had one.

"When they loaded the potatoes, did they weigh them by the basket or the whole wagon on a platform?"

"On a platform," I told him.

"Were you inside the building with the scale or were you outside?

"I was outside, sir."

"How do you know they had the correct weight?"

"I guess I don't."

"Is it possible the scale was off?

"Yes. The scale—"

"Because this is the second incident this week. Izio Z. was on duty there, and he had the same problem. Forty kilos missing."

60

"Okay. The scale must be wrong." That would be the official story. Everybody knew that Izio, a Sonder, was organizing more than I was. The inspector had been paid off. One hand washes the other. No one asked me about it again.

One hand washes the other. You did favors for those who could do favors for you. That's how a privileged class develops and is maintained. Like this: I was on duty, and this young guy, about my age, came to collect his ration of potatoes. This was a guy I wanted to help. I instructed the worker to shovel out a normal ration, which meant ten pounds or whatever the allowance was. It made a difference if you used a shovel or pitchfork, because the shovel brought more dirt and smaller potatoes from the pile, while the dirt and smallest potatoes fell off the fork. More dirt meant less weight in potatoes, and smaller potatoes were harder to peel. You lost more potato in the process. Such trivial things were not trivial in the ghetto. They were critical.

I asked the young guy, "Those potatoes okay?"

He wasn't impressed. "Well, that's the ration, so what can I do?"

"Dump them back on the pile, and let's go in the other room. I'll give you some real potatoes."

The other room had big, clean potatoes. Why didn't I take him there right away? I was doing him a favor, but I wanted to be sure he realized what a favor it was. See, he worked in a special distribution store where the food was better quality, and I wanted favorable treatment when I bought my special rations. That was the normal way of doing things. You made your connections and you got compensated. Having the right job made all the difference. I don't feel bad or good about it. That's just how it was.

The happiest moment—from my entire war experience—had to do with special rations. The super-privileged could buy certain delicacies, including sauerkraut, which was made in a cellar in the ghetto. One man supervised the sauerkraut production, directing the workers as they cut up cabbages and put them into barrels to cure. They used the white leaves of the cabbage and discarded the outer leaves and cores. I was on duty there once—naturally, a Sonder had to observe the operation—and a Sonder could take home all the scraps he could carry. If only I had a potato sack! If only I had known my assignment in advance. However, my grandparents' room in the hidden house was nearby, just across an old parking lot. And Grandfather had duffle bags left over from his leather goods shop—large canvas bags, like a seaman's bag, typically used for storing down comforters and pillows during summer. I

ANATOL CHARI & TIMOTHY BRAATZ

left my post and ran to the hidden house. It was a risk, but it was close to quitting time and an inspection was unlikely. The sauerkraut supervisor even suggested that I go. I returned with a bag and filled it with cabbage scraps. Stuffed it full. So full, so heavy, that I couldn't lift it. When the work day ended, a couple of guys helped me swing the bag onto my back. I climbed the three or four steps out of the cellar and dropped it. I couldn't carry it. I had to drag it home, through the mud. There had been snow, and the ground was wet and slippery, but so what? This was priceless treasure. When Grandmother opened the sack and saw her good fortune, how her family had been blessed, she was overjoyed. The expression on her face—I still remember it—was total happiness. That was *my* happiest moment, too. I've never seen anyone so happy. She would have fresh cabbage for several weeks for the evening soup, and that was just the beginning. Grandfather used most of the cabbage to make sauerkraut (rich in vitamin C, by the way), which would keep for months. Because of our positions—leather instructor and policeman—Grandfather and I received special rations. Add in the sauerkraut and the unmetered electricity, and we would be living comfortably the whole winter. You can see why Grandmother was elated.

Sometimes I could organize extra meat. Maybe you're thinking, "Why another food story?" All my stories are about food. During the war, that's all that mattered. There was a meat distribution store on the ground floor of the building where I had my own room. The store was only open two or three days a month, when meat was available. The building janitor was a butcher before the war, and he usually knew the guys who were sent to cut and distribute the meat. He also knew me—the Sonder who had guests all night—and, when I had guard duty in this meat store, he arranged an understanding. When the butchers weighed the rations, they would withhold a few grams here, a few grams there. Not enough that anyone would notice, but it added up. I would look the other way when they took their cut, and they would leave a kilo or two under the counter. After hours, the janitor and I would take that "extra" meat out the back door and divide it.

When we didn't have meat, Grandmother would make "hamburger" out of oats and barley flavored with a little onion or garlic or whatever there was. Call it a vegi-burger. When things were real tough, people made pancakes out of potato peels. It smelled so awful that I never ate it. You can make pancakes out of substitute coffee grounds. Also, inedible. In some rations, we got flour made from onion peels. It wouldn't absorb water. It was substitute sawdust. These things were inedible. To me, anyway. I could choose not to eat them. Whenever we had something just good enough to throw away, Grandfather would come home with a recipe for Grandmother. He would say, "Frume, I have a new way to make such-and-such." Whatever it was that day. "First, you boil the water. Then you add the onion peels, slowly, so it keeps boiling." Grandmother would be listening carefully, hoping the new recipe would make onion-peel flour tolerable. "After it boils a little—doesn't have to be too long—you carefully pour away the water. Next add fresh water and boil it for a half hour. Make sure to stir it. Then pour off the liquid and throw away the solids." Grandmother would fall for it every time.

Grandmother was naïve like that. She never really understood what was happening in the war. She even tried to keep kosher in the ghetto. Grandfather wasn't all that religious, but Grandmother was extremely devout. Her name, Frume, means "pious one." At the time she was born, when so many children died in infancy, parents chose names like Frume or Chaim ("life") or Alte ("old one") to fool the Angel of Death. Before the war, Grandmother had two stoves in the kitchen, one for meat dishes and one for dairy. She didn't have two stoves in the ghetto. She barely had one. But she did her best. Grandfather and I would bring home pig parts—ears and tails and such. The ghetto got the meat scraps considered unfit for German consumption—like throwing an unwanted bone to an unwanted dog—and it normally went to the special distribution stores. The general ghetto population was not dining on pig snouts. Yet Grandmother refused to eat the pork. In the beginning, anyway. Eventually, we convinced her it was like medicine—okay to eat if necessary for survival. Still, she would "kosher" her portion. She would salt it and put it in water, to draw out any blood, and then pretend it wasn't pork. She was a good woman. After the war, my cousin told me that in the ghetto, when he had visited Grandmother, she always offered him something to eat, even if it was only a piece of rutabaga. That's how she was.

I was close with my grandparents, and I became very close to Dorka Rabinovicz. She was about three years younger than me, a little bit shorter than me, and had brownish-blonde hair. I thought she was very pretty. We really liked each other. We would walk together for hours, just talking or not even talking, just holding hands. It was enough just being together. I asked my aunt, "Eva, how does it feel to fall in love?" I don't remember her answer. It didn't matter. I just felt comfortable with Dorka. I refer to her now as having been my fiancé. We weren't officially engaged, but she was my steady girlfriend. We were in love and together. People did get engaged and married in the ghetto. Motek, a friend from Rumkowski Gymnasium, and his wife, Wanda, consummated their marriage in my room. Well, almost. I returned home too soon. That was a week or two before they went to Auschwitz.

My best friend before the war was Kotek. His real name was Beno or Benjamin, but I started calling him Kotek—"little cat"—because the first time I went to his apartment they had a little cat. The name stuck. Before the war, we were classmates at Schweitzer Gymnasium, and, with a third friend, Heniek O., we often played cards at Kotek's apartment. In the ghetto, Kotek and I attended Rumkowski Gymnasium. We graduated together, became Sonders together, were privileged together. Heniek was a bright guy, a very quick learner—quicker than me—but didn't go to Rumkowski Gymnasium. Perhaps his family couldn't afford the tuition, and, of course, he didn't have the connection I had to the head Jew. Few did. Heniek didn't become a Sonder. He probably had a *ressort* job. Without special status, Heniek had to take bigger risks to organize food. He had to be creative. Yes, this story is about food. One night, Heniek snuck into a big distribution center. His plan was to fill a sack with potatoes, hide it in the bushes, and sneak out. He would return the next day with his family's ration cards and a second sack to buy their share of potatoes. Then he would recover the hidden potatoes and put them with the purchased potatoes. It was foolproof. He would exit through the checkpoint with a sack of potatoes and show his ration cards, like everybody else, only his sack would contain a lot more potatoes. If a guard got suspicious and had the potatoes reweighed, Heniek could claim that someone mistakenly gave him too many, that it wasn't his fault. Foolproof, except there were six or eight Sonders on night duty. They caught him sneaking in and surrounded him. I should say, *we* surrounded him. Fortunately for Heniek, Kotek and I were part of the guard detail that night. When I realized it was Heniek we were encircling, I quickly made a plan. I told Kotek to move over, make a space between the two of us, and I whispered to Heniek, "Get ready to run." I confiscated his sack and yelled at him, as I was expected to. I hit him, and he ran through the gap we had created and got away. Sonders wore boots with thick wooden soles. They were good protection from the cold. You could stand in the snow for three or four hours. But you couldn't run. There was no point in trying. The soles didn't flex and the snow stuck. You could barely walk. We could only watch Heniek disappear into the night. The other guys were suspicious.

"Why did you let him escape?"

"I didn't. He just dared to."

We put the potatoes back on the pile, and that was the end of it. End of part one of a two-part story. Thirty minutes later, I was standing alone at my post, and Heniek reappeared. He wanted the empty sack. If Heniek was turned in for organizing potatoes, he would be deported from the ghetto to who knows where. It wouldn't be good. But a sack for carrying potatoes or beets or other vegetables was very valuable in the ghetto and not easy to acquire. As Grandmother used to say, "*Nie tak szkoda, jak wygoda*"—It's not so much the loss as the convenience of having the thing," or maybe "It's not valuable, but you can't replace it."

Again to show you my special status, Heniek was risking his life for an empty potato sack while I was the very proud owner of leather riding boots. When I became a Sonder, I wanted riding boots—a real status symbol in the ghetto, worth maybe six pounds of flour. That's expensive. My grandfather organized some leather from the *ressort* where he worked, and I must have traded bread or potatoes for some additional pieces. Then we took the leather to a shoemaker. I only wore the riding boots two or three times. They were very uncomfortable. The first time I wore them to work, the lieutenants didn't say anything, but they soon assigned me to internal duty, where I couldn't organize food, as a sort of penalty because anyone with new boots obviously had organized food to pay for them. I probably paid the shoemaker half a loaf of bread. I still remember going to see him. It was dark, probably about six in the evening, and the shoemaker and his son were in their small room, sitting on a bench facing each other. Between them was a large soup pot. We asked what they were eating, and they explained that without someone to cook for them, they would share one midday soup at work and save the other for dinner. To make the dinner soup go further, they would add water. I had seen a lot of deprivation, yet this struck me as very sad. They were adding water to what was already mostly water. The point was to have a full belly to sleep on. The shoemaker's wife had died in typical ghetto fashion—malnutrition and, consequently, tuberculosis—and there they sat eating water for dinner. I felt sorry for them.

There were a lot of sad things in the ghetto, a lot of people to feel sorry for, and some moments still affect me over sixty years later. I was on night duty at one of the big vegetable distribution places. There were probably fifteen Sonders there. You had three cold hours outside at one of the six guard posts, then three hours sleeping inside. On this particular night, I had outdoor duty from two to five in the morning. Something like that. When I got to the gate, there was a young woman, about my age, standing at the fence. It was winter and very cold.

"What are you doing?" I asked.

"They're distributing the new potato rations tomorrow, and if I'm first in line I can get the potatoes and still make it to work in time for the midday soup."

You have to understand, there were two large distribution centers for potatoes and vegetables. One was on the corner next to the church on Łagiewnicka Street and the other was across the street from my apartment. The food arrived on the train at Marysin, was taken to the storage fields, and then brought to these two centers. Two distribution centers for tens of thousands of ghetto residents, so you can imagine the lines. Privileged people like me could go to two or three special rations stores without lines. The super-privileged probably had food delivered to their apartments. The average person, like this young woman, might have to stand in line half the day if she didn't arrive early. Well, she had arrived very early.

"Do you know what time it is?" I asked her.

"No, I—"

"It's two o'clock. You have five hours until they open. Why don't you go home?"

"No, I'll wait."

"You're going to stand here all night?"

"Well, I'm already here." I can still see her standing at the fence—no one to go home to, and nothing better to do. It was sad.

The saddest moment of all came when I was guarding a field of vegetables grown for the super-elites, for people like Rumkowski and his council, department heads, and stool pigeons. When the fieldworkers gathered the vegetables, they could keep leaves and things, the throwaways.[46] A woman, maybe thirty years old, came by in the evening, around closing time. She carried a bag and asked the foreman if she could get some throwaway greens for soup. He had nothing to give her. The workers, he explained, hadn't picked anything that day. There were no scraps. When she heard this, her arms sagged at her sides. I can still see her, her disappointment, a picture of disillusionment. She didn't speak a word, but

---

[46] In July, 1942, a very hungry Dawid Sierakowiak wrote, "Radish leaves are our essential food." Sierakowiak, *The Diary*, 194.

her face said, What am I going to feed to my children? How am I going to tell them there is nothing to eat? That still affects me. When my father was taken away, I didn't realize it was the final goodbye. The Gestapo men were polite. I wasn't scared. I didn't fully understand the situation that was developing in Łódź. I felt sadder when I saw the sadness in this woman. I understood the situation, and so did she.

At the time, I felt sorry for these people just trying to survive. Today, looking back, I feel that as a Sonder—a privileged guy who supervised food distribution and easily organized some for myself—I participated in creating the situation, and I feel especially guilty about the people I didn't help. Sins of omission. One evening, Tola came to my apartment, woke me up, and crawled into my bed. She wanted me to go downstairs and collect her ration at the meat store before it closed. She had a ration card, but, as a Sonder who knew the workers there, I wouldn't have to wait in the long line outside and I could get better meat, not just trimmings. I refused. I was real tired from being on duty all day. I didn't even feel like fooling around with her, so I must have been fatigued, but I could have managed to walk down the stairs. She was counting on me and I did nothing. I let her down. No, I didn't increase her suffering, but I didn't ease it either. That still bothers me. The organizing doesn't bother me. You did that to survive. But not helping someone when I could have—that's what nags at me to this day. If Tola were still alive, if I knew where she was, I would go and ask forgiveness. I can't forgive myself. The millions that died in the gas chambers—that doesn't nag at me. That wasn't my doing. This one was. Why didn't I go downstairs for her? Was it fatigue or indifference? Also, the poor woman who couldn't get any throwaway greens. Grandmother was so happy with a bag-full of throwaway greens, and the woman who got nothing was devastated. I could have done something for her. Or the time I was on duty, watching the midday soup distribution at a clothing *ressort*, and I saw a girl I knew, a classmate from Rumkowski Gymnasium. She looked at me. Her expression said, "Do something for me." I told the soup server to give her a better soup, take it from the bottom of the pot, but I could have done more. It still bothers me that I didn't tell the girl to come back at closing time for another soup. You know, alleviate her suffering just a little. I feel guilty about that even though I know she survived the war. I'm sure there are some other things I could have done to help someone and didn't, could have given an extra soup or some potato peels. In normal times, these little omissions may not be worth mentioning—"No, I don't have time to do that for you"—but looking back at the dire circumstances of the ghetto, they carry more weight.

Most Sonders who survived the war don't admit to having been ghetto policemen. We had it so much better than most in the ghetto, and it's hard not to feel guilty. Many resented us and our privilege.[47] At the time, no one said anything to you. There was nothing to be ashamed of, nothing to hide. It was just a fact of life. You're a policeman or you're a factory manager and you're better off. That's just the way it is. Not so different from today. After the war, though, some people saw us as collaborators. We were working for the Germans after all, doing the policing for them. But anyone who survived the ghetto was working for the Germans. To survive you had to eat, and to eat you had to work. There was no way around it. And the work was intended, in one way or another, to support the German war effort. I don't see the difference between the policeman supervising soup distribution in a shoe *ressort*, the kitchen worker ladling out the soup, and the *ressort* worker making straw shoes for the German army, except that the soup server was eating more than the shoemaker, and the policeman was eating better than both. Yes, some had it easier. Yes, I had chances to help people and I didn't. That's what I feel guilty about. I'm not claiming to be innocent of selfish behavior. But everyone was trying to survive as best they could under conditions not meant for survival. I'll say it again, if you only ate the standard allotment of food, you weren't going to live. If you did live, if you made it through the ghetto, and through the camps after the ghetto, if you came out alive, then you couldn't have been among the worst off in the ghetto. If you really had it bad, you're not here to tell about it. The sick and malnourished ghetto deportees didn't last long in the even worse conditions of the camps, and, anyway, the Germans usually gassed those people immediately. I resent it when I hear survivors claim they made it through without any relative privilege, or that they were somehow innocent of selfish behavior. It's not true.

What is true is that we in the elite class were living in a kind of fantasy world. Especially the ones my age—getting dressed up, having get-togethers, carrying on as if life was normal. The Germans didn't control our lives minute by minute like they did in the camps, so you could pretend your life

[47] Sierkowiak, *The Diary*, 248-249, complained that the Sonders controlled "almost the entire food-distribution system in the ghetto now," and that they "feed themselves as much as they wish, and live the good life, while the gray mass of the 'unconnected' population...."

was normal. Maybe for us it was. Maybe we were too young to really understand. We were totally locked in, isolated. We had no concept of what was happening outside the fence. Meanwhile, inside the fence, people were starving and people were being killed by the Kripo and people were being transported to God knows where, and yet the elite girls were wearing fancy hats and putting on make-up. In the middle of the Holocaust, I arranged for riding boots. Can you imagine? While others were dreaming of getting a bowl of soup, I was hoping I would someday have a silk shirt. When I look at the photograph of my class on graduation day at Rumkowski Gymnasium, I have to wonder about how we took ourselves so seriously in our substitute life.

And I have to admit, there was a level of deprivation in the ghetto that I wasn't aware of or just refused to be aware of. One time I pulled a guy out of line at the distribution place below my room. I was on duty, and this woman started screaming, "That guy doesn't belong here. He just pushed his way in." He was a head taller than me, but when I grabbed him by the coat, he fell like a piece of paper. He had no energy. It scared me how lifeless he was. So I should have known how bad it could be. I knew people were dying in the ghetto. But many years later, in the 1990s, I read the diary of Dawid Sierakowiak. The ghetto schools were closed just before Dawid entered the lyceum, so he never graduated. A few years older, he probably would have been in my class and would have become a Sonder. Instead, when I read his story, it seemed like he and I had been on different planets. Toward the end of the diary, before he died of disease and malnutrition, he was writing mostly about getting, or not getting, an extra soup. While I was dreaming about one day having a silk shirt, he was living from one soup to the next. I was totally shocked when I read this. I never realized that people had it so bad—it never occurred to me—and I saw them every day.[48]

Earlier, I said there was no public transportation in the ghetto, but there was a streetcar line. At one end, it stopped at the train station in Marysin, where food came in and people went out. The streetcar was not for general movement around the ghetto. There was just one car, and it pulled two flatbeds behind it. It was used to bring food from Marysin to the distribution centers in the center of town, and to take people to the train station to board

---

[48] Sierakowiak was trying desperately to become a Sonder. On March 30, 1943, he wrote, "Admission to the Sonderabteilung is almost the only chance I have to save my health!" He died in August. Sierakowiak, *The Diary*, 264.

the transports. For many of them, it was the beginning of the end. Once, I took Dorka for a ride on the streetcar. When we jumped on, the conductor began to protest. We weren't allowed on the car. I flipped over my lapel and showed him my police badge, and that was that. We rode from the big distribution center in town to Marysin, to where there were no buildings, only fields, and took a walk. It was like that for us. We lived in a kind of denial. I'm not saying life was pleasant. I can remember lying on my bed, smoking a cigarette, after a long day on duty. Looking out my window, I could see only stars, and I thought to myself, "We got stuck in the ghetto, the worst place in the world." The denial was refusing to believe it could get worse for us. We told ourselves that we wouldn't be deported, that life would remain like this until the Germans lost and the war ended. We had to believe the Germans would lose. It was our only hope. We would keep having our get-togethers, keep organizing extra potatoes, keep living, and then one day the victorious Russians would arrive and open the gates. That's not exactly how it went for us. Our fantasy world of ghetto privilege was long gone by the time the Germans surrendered.

3

AUSCHWITZ

In August, 1944, the Germans liquidated the Łódź ghetto.[49] What does that mean? It means the Russian army was getting closer. It means, with defeat a real possibility, the Germans transported the ghetto population westward to Auschwitz for extermination. We had some sense the Russians were making progress from the east. There were maybe four or five radios in the ghetto, hidden from the Germans. Polish and German civilians occasionally came into the ghetto to confer with the heads of the gas and electrical departments, and occasionally they brought in a newspaper and "forgot" to take it out. It wasn't much, but the radios and occasional newspaper allowed a little bit of news to circulate in the ghetto. Two or three days after the Normandy invasion, we knew something was going on. After that, though, the Germans tried to crack down.[50] The Kripo arrested two guys for having radios. One was the barber who cut my hair. Neither returned from the Kripo interrogation. But there were others. My friend Maniek R., the guy who first rigged my electricity, had a radio. Someone must have denounced him to Rumkowski's administration, maybe said that Maniek was talking about news reports. But the Jewish police who investigated knew Maniek and his family. They told him, "Tell us where the radio is so we don't look there." So a few radios remained, and they brought

---

[49] Liquidation began in June, 1944, but was halted in July after the Chelmno death camp was closed, then resumed in August with transports to Auschwitz. Dobroszycki, *The Chronicle*, lxiii.

[50] Dobroszycki, *The Chronicle*, lxv, notes, "On the day after Allied forces landed at Normandy (D-Day), there were large-scale arrests of those listening to radios in the ghetto."

hope. The Normandy invasion was too far to the west to matter much. What mattered were reports of where the Germans were winning in the east. It helped to know the geography. The reports were always that the Germans were winning, only you would notice that previously they were winning near Kiev and now they were winning by Charków. They were winning in the wrong direction. The Russians were on their way! I didn't get excited. It had taken the Germans two years to fight to Moscow, and I figured it would probably take just as long for the Russians to push them back. I told people, "Don't expect them here next week." But the ghetto lived on rumors. This is happening. That is happening. The next ration of potatoes is going to be six kilos. Right. You believed it because it kept the spirit up. At night, we played cards by moonlight and we said such things. It's going to be better in another week. In another month it will be over. You convinced yourself there was hope.

Maybe we were lying to ourselves, but Hans Biebow, the German administrator responsible for the ghetto, definitely lied to us about liquidation. As I understand it, Biebow tried for as long as he could to prevent elimination of the ghetto, tried to keep authorities in Berlin convinced that our labor was crucial to the war effort. He was making money off the ghetto, and the job kept him off the Russian front. He probably thought it was easier to fight the Jews than the Russians.[51] However, when the order for liquidation was given, he had to oversee it. He gave a speech, assuring us on his honor as a German officer that we were being relocated for labor purposes.[52] The transports will be organized by *ressort*, Biebow said. All the workers from a *ressort* will go together, and we'll ship the factory materials after you. The workers only needed to number their stools and machines. That way, he explained, when the workers reached their destination, they could quickly reassemble their workplace and not lose productivity. It was a better story, I suppose, than we are sending you to Auschwitz to annihilate you.

When I heard about the speech, when I realized that the whole ghetto was going, I had a bad feeling about it. For the past two and a half years, the

---

[51] Dobroszycki, *The Chronicle*, xli-xlii, explains, "The post of head of the ghetto administration may have seemed very lucrative to [Biebow], and it also exempted him from military service and, later on, from going to the front."

[52] In the first week of August, 1944, Biebow gave several speeches assuring ghetto residents that "every worker is to be used in the war effort" and they would go in family units to new work camps. Adelson and Lapides, *Łódź Ghetto*, 438 and 441; Trunk, *Łódź Ghetto*, 290-291.

Germans had been deporting people from the ghetto. There were many transports, not just the infamous ones of 1942 when the Germans took thousands at a time. For example, whenever the ghetto jail was full, the Gestapo would empty it out, putting five hundred or so on a train. We didn't know where the transports went, we didn't know about gas vans and gas chambers, so a person could pretend it was just a new work assignment. However, if you thought about it honestly—which we rarely did—you knew it couldn't be good. The Germans had selected the elderly, the young, and the visibly weak. They took people from the insane asylum and the hospitals. That doesn't seem like labor recruitment. And privileged people weren't selected. Policemen didn't go. Foreign Jews who had served in the Kaiser's military during the previous war—decorated veterans—were also exempt. Clearly, whatever it meant, selection for transport was not desirable.

There were other clues. Shipments of used clothing arrived in the ghetto, and Sonders supervised the girls who sorted the shirts and coats and things, making sure they didn't pocket any valuables they might find. We didn't realize the clothing was coming back from the previous transports. We didn't let ourselves realize it. One day, in early 1944, I was on this clothing duty and I saw six shirts together. Six blood-soaked shirts with the same bullet hole. Because they were only allowed one suitcase or package, the transportees would wear all the clothing they owned, whatever it was—two suits, a heavy coat, a raincoat, two hats, and lots of shirts. Nobody wanted to put two and two together, but buried in the subconscious, somewhere, you knew the guy who was shot had exited the ghetto wearing six shirts. The blood belonged to a deported Jew.

As a Sonder, I had helped with these earlier transports. The Gestapo demanded a certain number of people—five hundred, twelve thousand, whatever it was—and Rumkowski's administration drew up a list of names. If you were on the list, you were supposed to pack your bag and report to the Krawiecka Street jail.[53] If you didn't report, the ghetto policemen and firemen went from room to room looking for you. There would be a total curfew until the German's quota was filled. The *ressorts* were closed. Everyone was supposed to be home at their assigned address. I remember going into a room where a brother and sister lived. They slept in the same bed, without sheets. Just a single blanket and a pillow. I told the brother,

---

[53] The Central Prison was located at 12 Krawiecka Street. Dobroszycki, *The Chronicle*, 506.

"You come with us." There was no bargaining, no "why me?" He just came, leaving his sister behind. We took him to the police station or wherever the gathering place was. I felt very bad for his sister, all alone now, and the bed even colder. The rest of her family was already dead. It was sad. If I could have taken someone instead of her brother, I would have.

During one such deportation, I had night duty, so I was home during the day when the search party came through my building. The guy who knocked on my door was a Sonder who knew me. "Oh," he said, "we didn't know you lived here." They didn't search my room. They didn't find my friend Lutek under the bed. Lutek was a baker, a worker deemed "unessential" to the war effort, and his name was on the list, so I let him hide in my room. Celinka was another likely candidate. She, too, had an "unessential" job, and she lived alone—no children to tend, the rest of her family probably gone. Celinka asked to hide in my room, and I refused her. There wasn't enough room for both her and Lutek. If someone came to the door, we would all be exposed. My conscience still bothers me about that. Celinka was picked up and deported, probably to Chelmno or Belzec for immediate disposal. I should have helped her. Maybe she could have squeezed under the bed with Lutek. He escaped selection and survived the war. You see, after the round-up, it was safe to go back to work, even if you had been on the list. Once the transport left, no one looked for you. The Gestapo's demands had been fulfilled—for the moment. Later, during liquidation, Lutek went to Auschwitz like everybody else, then was sent to Buchenwald. He was a handsome guy—blue eyes, blonde hair—and one day at Buchenwald he decided he'd had enough of being a Jew. He somehow changed his camp uniform markings from the Jewish star to a red triangle and became a Polish political prisoner. After the war, after he was liberated by the Allies, he became a Jew again.

Then there was Anita. I don't remember how I met her. We fooled around some, but I never slept with her. She would come to visit me while I was on night duty guarding the fields where vegetables were grown for the elites. I'm not sure what her job was. When the war began, she had papers that allowed her to pass as a non-Jew. The Germans sent her with other Polish girls to a forced labor camp in Germany. The other girls were jealous of Anita because she was the mistress of the German camp commandant, and they threatened to expose her as a Jew. When the rumors reached the commandant, he promised her safe passage back to Poland, to the Łódź ghetto, if she confessed to being a Jew. She got scared and, stupidly, told him the truth. He kept his promise. Maybe if she had come to the ghetto earlier she would have found "essential" work. Instead, like Celinka, she went on one of the transports, probably to be gassed.

And there was Norbert. In school, before the war, we called him Schwabik—the little Schwab. That meant, "the little German," and wasn't entirely complimentary—like calling someone in the US a "Kraut." His family had lived in Berlin, but, in 1934 or 1935, when Germany became dangerous for Jews, they moved to Łódź. Although they had Polish-Jewish origins, they didn't speak a word of Polish when they arrived. They were what Germans called "dirty eastern Jews." That's not entirely complimentary either. I saw Norbert again in the ghetto, in early 1944, behind barbed wire. He had reported to the holding area to await transport. I went over to talk to him. He told me, "I'm sick of running. I can't anymore."

When the Germans began the total liquidation, they used the ghetto policemen and firemen to keep people moving. The firemen were used because, like Sonders, they wore uniforms. The transports were organized by *ressort*, but if a *ressort* didn't have enough workers to fill a train and there weren't enough family members and other volunteers to go with them, the Germans would round up more people.[54] The Sonders, myself included, helped them. I can remember leading a group of sixty or so deportees to the gathering place. Two other policemen were assisting, and a German followed in the rear. I knew one of the deportees, a baker, and he approached me.

"Mr. Sonder, let me go home, okay? I want to go in the transport tomorrow with my family."

"Alright. Here we turn right. You go straight. Don't run."

I let him go, and the German supervisor either didn't notice or didn't give a damn. If the Jew doesn't die today, he'll die tomorrow, so what difference does it make?

It took three or four weeks to liquidate the ghetto. You can't evacuate one hundred thousand people—or however many were left—in a day.[55] Sonders were working overtime. I guarded food distribution during the day, then had partial night duty collecting people for the trains. After a few hours

---

[54] As liquidation proceeded, more and more ghetto residents hid from the round-ups, so armed German firemen and policemen entered the ghetto, surrounded entire blocks, and ordered Jewish policemen to drag people from their hiding places. Dobroszycki, *The Chronicle*, lxv.

[55] The final liquidation lasted from August 3 to 28, 1944. When it began, the ghetto population was down to around 68,000. Dobroszycki, *The Chronicle*, lxiv-lxv.

sleep, I was back on day duty. I discovered that if you propped a shovel against a fence and leaned against the shovel, you could sleep standing up.

As the trains came and went, we gained some sense of where ghetto residents were being sent. The trains left filled with people and their few possessions. When the trains returned empty, workers went in to clean out the cars. They found notes that read, "We are at Auschwitz. It's not good." Before the war, Auschwitz had been a small Polish town in the middle of nowhere. Most people in Łódź had never even heard of it, so "Auschwitz" meant nothing to us. "Not good" was ominous. Worse than the ghetto? Still, with everyone leaving, and the neighborhoods emptying, it became desirable to go. Maybe it wouldn't be so bad. After all, the Germans had said to take your valuables and carefully mark your luggage so it doesn't get lost. And they were letting us go in families. Besides, what else could you do? Where could you hide? There was no resistance to speak of. In the Warsaw ghetto, the resistance had used the sewer system to bring in weapons and sneak people out, and they had help from the Polish resistance. The Łódź ghetto had no sewer system, and the local Polish population was no help. Early on, some young people in a communist organization in the ghetto had tried to organize work sabotage. One organizer was the son of a very privileged man, the head of a metal *ressort*. When the son tried to organize a strike, the father pointed out that the workers didn't have such privileges as heating and extra food, and maybe the son should join the workers instead of eating at home. That ended the son's involvement, and the sabotage never amounted to anything.[56] There was submission to orders from above. You had to work to eat. That's just how it was. And if you're passive long enough, you become passive forever. When the liquidation began, then, most people just went along, hoping the ghetto would somehow be re-created, with *ressorts* and families intact .

My fiancé Dorka came to my place late one night to tell me she was leaving in the morning with the transport of court workers. There were two courts in the ghetto. The Sonders ran a court that wasn't really official. There were no lawyers or judges, just three or four lieutenants who spoke German (they were from either Germany or Czechoslovakia) and were very lenient. They might sentence someone to three days cleaning floors. They

---

[56] Ghetto residents did engage in food riots, work slowdowns and stoppages, and protests against the ghetto administration, and there was a movement of politicized young people, but no organized resistance to German rule developed. Trunk, *Łódź Ghetto*, 325-332.

didn't send people to the ghetto jail. The official court was part of Rumkowski's administration. For minor offenses, this court might punish you with outhouse detail. For major crimes, like organizing food, they would sentence the offender to the jail, which meant going on the next transport, effectively a death sentence. My cousin Moniek P., a lawyer before the war, was a judge on the court. Dorka's two sisters worked in the court, and her brother was also somehow involved. I don't remember Dorka's job. She was from a privileged family, so it couldn't have been difficult work. Anyhow, she was leaving with her brother and sisters and the rest of the court workers. I suggested she wait a few days and we could go together. "No, I'll go with my family. I'll see you there." We said goodbye, and I never saw her again.

I don't think I ever said goodbye to my stepmother. She and her family—what was left of it—her sister Hella and Hella's son—went to Auschwitz on the day before I did. The entire transport was probably gassed upon arrival. I never really said goodbye to my grandparents, either. About a week before being deported, they were locked into the leather *ressort* where they worked and isolated from the rest of the ghetto. The Germans still considered them "essential" to the war effort, and didn't want "unessential" workers sneaking into their group. The closed group of leather workers went on transport after I did, and I never saw my grandparents at Auschwitz.

The transport of policemen and firemen went two or three nights after the court workers. We were among the last. A few days earlier, Sergeant G. came to me with a proposal. Sergeant G. was the Don Juan who swapped stories of conquest with Lutek that night in the bakery. He had found a double cellar. The first cellar was below street level by three or four steps, and the floor was covered with maybe a foot of water. You walked through it to the next cellar, which was a few feet higher and dry. Sergeant G.'s idea was that the two of us would organize some food and hide in the second cellar for a week or two to avoid deportation. The water in the first cellar would prevent the Gestapo's dogs from sniffing us out. We could stay hidden, he believed, until the Germans quit looking for stragglers. He told me where the cellar was and how we would get the necessary food. I declined, and he decided not to do it alone. Could we have made it? In the end, we would have crawled out of the cellar in search of more food, and probably would have been caught by the Germans or the Russians. Neither option was good. The Germans would have shot us. The Russians probably would have identified us as Sonders and sent us to Siberia as punishment for collaborating with the Germans.

There was one chance, though. The Germans didn't deport every single person from the ghetto to Auschwitz. I know that a few privileged German Jews, like Rumkowski's secretary, were sent to a camp in Germany. The secretary was from Cologne, and after the war I heard she was back there. Some of the super-privileged, like the head of the electrical department, were never evacuated at all because the Germans still needed them in Łódź.[57] Another one was Mozelsio, a leather tanner. Before the war, he ran his own tannery. When the Germans arrived, they needed his expertise. Once or twice a week, he took off his jacket with the Jewish star and went with the Gestapo to inspect the Łódź tanneries and advise on production plans. His son, Kuba, was a few years behind me in school before the war. Talk about privileged, the Germans never confiscated the Mozelsio family's possessions, and Kuba had a bicycle in the ghetto. That was like a high-schooler today owning a Porsche. The family was spared deportation, and many years after the war, through a mutual acquaintance, Kuba gave me some pre-war pictures of my school days. I'm not sure if these people who weren't deported continued to live in the same Baluty apartments and neighborhoods after the ghetto was liquidated, but some were still in Łódź when the Russians arrived five months later.[58]

The White Guard also remained behind. The Germans retained seven hundred of these able-bodied men to gather up anything of value, like clothing or furniture, left in the ghetto. For three months, the White Guard lived in barracks and were supervised by a Jew named Bruder, who had been a noncommissioned officer in the German or Austrian army during World War I.[59] Bruder understood German, and he overheard the Gestapo men discussing their plan to shoot the White Guard once the work was completed. When the Gestapo went to the barracks to carry this out, the White Guard had disappeared. They were hiding in the Marysin cemetery, and the Russians were so close that the Gestapo didn't have time to search for them.[60] When

---

[57] According to the diary of Jakub Poznanski, about five hundred ghetto elites, including Engineer Weinberg, were kept behind. Adelson and Lapides, *Łódź Ghetto*, 457-478. Many of them were deported to work camps in Germany on October 21, 1944. Dobroszycki, *The Chronicle*, lxvi, n168.

[58] When the Soviets arrived in January, 1945, they found 877 ghetto residents still alive. Trunk, *Łódź Ghetto*, xi.

[59] According to the Poznanski diary, Bruder, the "chief of the Jewish police," was put in charge of the remaining Jews on December 3, 1944. Adelson and Lapides, *Łódź Ghetto*, 481-482.

[60] Poznanski's diary explains that on the evening of January 17, 1945, after Commander Bruder announced a mandatory roll call for the following day, the remaining ghetto

the Russians arrested Bruder for collaboration, his White Guard subordinates testified that he had been looking out for them, and he was released. A few other ghetto residents had gone into hiding like Sergeant G. suggested he and I do. The Germans normally shot them on sight, but did put a few to work with the White Guard.[61] Maybe the Gestapo would have assigned Sergeant G. and me to the White Guard. Maybe no one would have denounced us as Sonders when the Russians arrived. Big maybe's. That would have been our only chance. As it turned out, Sergeant G. didn't survive the war.

What about Rumkowski? What became of the Eldest of the Jews? He was sent to Auschwitz and went straight to the crematorium complex, where he was killed.[62] The story goes that the crematorium workers showed him some corpses, told him he was responsible, then burned him alive. No one knows if that's true or if he was gassed. Rumkowski is a controversial figure. In some books, he is depicted as an absolute monster. That depends on which side of the coin you were. If you never got to see him and he never did you a favor and just by rare chance you still made it, then he was a tyrant. He cooperated with the Germans. Which is true—he did as he was told. But when you were in a position like I was, he was also a human being. Anybody who had it good will tell you that Rumkowski did all he could to preserve the ghetto. He kept the Gestapo from taking over his job and doing worse. His goal was to save at least some Jews, even at the expense of others. He tried to save those to whom he felt an obligation because of previous connections and also those he thought would be beneficial to a Jewish future. He wanted us, the educated ones, to survive. That's who he chose. He made us a privileged class. I'm not saying he was right doing what he did this way or that way. I'm not saying he saved every deserving person. Every person deserved to be saved.

However, the situation could have played out differently, had a different ending, and then maybe Rumkowski would be viewed differently. If there

residents went into hiding. Nine mass graves had been dug in the Jewish cemetery. "We know that the Germans plan to slaughter us before they leave Łódź." Adelson and Lapides, *Łódź Ghetto*, 485-487. The Germans fled on January 18, and Soviet troops arrived on January 20. There were 877 Jews still in the ghetto, including the White Guard. Dobroszycki, *The Chronicle*, lxvi.

[61] Poznanski mentions Jews found hiding who were beaten, then sent to join the work crews. Adelson and Lapides, *Łódź Ghetto*, 467.

[62] Rumkowski went on one of the last transports—on August 28, 1944. Dobroszycki, *The Chronicle*, lxv. The circumstances of his death remain unclear. Adelson and Lapides, *Łódź Ghetto*, 493.

hadn't been a Polish uprising in Warsaw, and if the Russians hadn't halted their advance, maybe the Łódź ghetto wouldn't have been liquidated.[63] At Kraków, the Russians came so quickly, without a fight or bombing, that they found warm food on the table. The German occupiers had fled without carrying out any final actions. Without the delay at Warsaw, maybe Łódź would have been like Kraków—suddenly captured by the Russian army—and the majority of the ghetto population would have survived. That's strictly speculation, though, because the Germans could have sped up the liquidation in Łódź by two or three months if they had wanted. They could have had death marches. But maybe the better ending is what Rumkowski was planning for—hoping for—the Germans fleeing Łódź without clearing the ghetto. I don't know if the people who criticize him would have done any better in his situation. I get plenty annoyed with survivors who claim to have made it without any privileges, without cooperating, without doing anything that others, looking back, might consider unethical. Everyone cooperated—the question is only of extent. Did you just work, or did you make others work too, and was that right?

I don't want to judge Rumkowski one way or the other. I know I'm biased toward him. In the 1990s, Lolek C. and I were walking together through Washington, D.C., on our way to the National Holocaust Museum. I was complaining to him that Rumkowski doesn't get enough credit for saving as many Jews as he did. When we were sent to Auschwitz, it was out of Rumkowski's hands, but more Jews from Łódź survived the war than from all the other ghettos put together. Rumkowski must have been thinking of the future because he started a *hafshara* in the ghetto. This was a facility for study of agricultural arts, like sheep-raising (though we had no sheep), to prepare students for kibbutz life in Israel after the war. It was part of Rumkowski Gymnasium. I didn't attend the *hafshara*, but Lolek did. Lolek was with me in Rumkowski Gymnasium, in the gasworks, and in the Sonders. In the ghetto, he was in the privileged class. Yet my privileges were greater still. The Eldest of the Jews was personally looking out for me. Now, some fifty years after the war, as Lolek and I walked to the museum and I complained about

---

[63] Soviet forces reached the eastern bank of the Vistula River, opposite Warsaw, in the last week of July, 1944. On August 1, an armed uprising against the Germans began in Warsaw. The Soviets stayed outside the city, allowing the Germans to destroy the nationalist resistance, then resumed the offensive in January, 1945. Norman Davies, *Rising '44: The Battle for Warsaw* (New York: Penguin, 2004), 163-165, 314-322.

Rumkowski's disrepute, Lolek remarked, "Tolek, don't forget, you had *special* privileges."

When I got off the train in Auschwitz, those special privileges came to a sudden end. Getting on the train, I didn't have any particular attitude. We were just going somewhere, though I knew it couldn't be good. We left Łódź in the evening and arrived at Auschwitz in the early morning. It must have been about an eight-hour trip, traveling almost directly south. We went in cattle cars, with maybe one hundred in a car. It was late summer, and the car had an open window, crossed with barbed wire, so it wasn't totally uncomfortable. Not exactly shackles or something like that. Remember, "I don't have it so bad" is a state of mind that depends on what you're accustomed to, your expectations, and understanding that others have it worse. On the transport, you could rest your head on your luggage, and I was used to sleeping on wood, so it wasn't so bad. We went near the area where I used to spend summer with my cousins, and I thought, "If I could jump out of the train, perhaps one of the farmers would remember me." It didn't really seem possible. I just had the thought.

After eight hours or whatever, the train slowed down and stopped, then started again. There was some shifting back and forth. The sun was already up, and through the cattle car's window you could see signs reading "Auschwitz." We saw people in striped uniforms like pajamas. They looked emaciated. Very emaciated. They shouted, "Throw us some bread. They're going to take it from you anyway." Nobody threw them bread. We didn't comprehend what we saw. This must have been the point when the earlier transportees had written their warning notes and hidden them in the cars. They had written that "Auschwitz" looked bad. Well, now I was there, and it did look bad—the prisoners looked awful—but the train hadn't completely stopped. It kept going back and forth, starting and stopping, before the gate, through the gate, probably trying to align properly on the tracks. I hoped we weren't stopping. I hoped we were going somewhere else. That feeling stayed with me a long time. After the war, even after I had moved to the United States, I would be riding a train—say, from Rochester to New York City—and I would be hoping that I would never arrive, that the train would just keep going. When I took the Greyhound bus from Rochester to Chicago, I wanted it to continue. I didn't want to get off the bus. I'm over it now—the fear of getting there, wherever *there* is—but it lasted for years.

Then the banging on the train doors started, the doors opened, and we heard, "Out, out, out! Women this way. Men that way. Leave your luggage behind." It was total terror from the first moment—the yelling and screaming, the disorientation. We were separated from our possessions and herded down the ramp. I had brought my most valuable possession, my pride and joy...my riding boots. Can you imagine, bringing uncomfortable riding boots to Auschwitz? I had to leave them in the cattle car. The privileged life of a Sonder was over.

The directions were coming from experienced prisoners who worked at the train platform. This work detail was called "Canada"—don't ask me why—and included political and criminal prisoners from Germany and Poland and also Jewish prisoners.[64] They yelled and hit us and told us where to stand, then herded the women toward two or three German officers for the selection. While the women went through, the men stood waiting and terrified as the yelling and hitting continued. Then it was our turn. We filed past the officers, who told you either go left or go right. I could tell that the younger and healthier ones were being directed one way and the sick and elderly the other way. Somehow I knew it was better to be sent with the healthier group, which I was. I had come to Auschwitz at a "good" time. The Germans had an acute labor shortage. They were no longer indiscriminately gassing people who were fit enough to dig ditches. When I passed through the selection, the German officers could see that I wasn't completely exhausted. I was still useful. They could still squeeze some labor out of me before I dropped dead. All that extra food I got as a Sonder had, for the moment, saved me. The less healthy ones, I now know, were headed straight to the gas chamber. The "Canada" workers were being very polite to the condemned ones, telling them to take their time, trying not to scare them into panic or resistance. There was even a truck to carry those too weak to walk.

I can only guess at the numbers. I would say there were one hundred in a cattle car, and twenty to thirty cars on our transport. So two to three thousand people, and maybe seventy percent on our train went to the gas chamber. Just a guess. If you read books about Auschwitz, about people who were in Auschwitz, almost no one mentions the transports from Łódź. To the resident Auschwitz prisoners, we weren't noteworthy. We didn't bring food or nice clothing with us like the French and Belgium Jews did. We

---

[64] The workers at the ramp hauled away the new arrivals' luggage, and they "associated the sheer amount of loot and its mind-boggling value with the riches symbolized by Canada." Yisrael Gutman and Michael Berenbaum, eds., *Anatomy of the Auschwitz Death Camp* (Bloomington: Indiana University Press, 1998), 250-251.

didn't join the resident population. We didn't displace anyone. Maybe one hundred thousand came from Łódź when the ghetto was liquidated, but we were insignificant in the annals of Auschwitz. Just a drop in the bucket.

Since I wasn't chosen for the gas, I was directed to walk down the railroad tracks. I was with another Sonder and his brother. I don't remember their names. On the train, I had been lying next to the Sonder. A very good-looking guy. He told me that during the night, while most on the train were sleeping, he had screwed the girl who was lying to his other side. They had just met in the cattle car. Last chance, I guess. We walked together down the tracks for ten or fifteen minutes. There were no guards. The Sonder took off his watch. "I'm not giving this to them," he said, and slammed it on the ground.

"What was that?" asked an SS man who was coming up the tracks.

"A broken watch. It was broken." The SS man let him go.

We were headed for the "sauna," the main shower area for prisoners not to be gassed. We were standing outside—men and women—I don't know how many. When we left the ghetto, the Germans had told us to bring our valuables along. Now we learned it wasn't for safe-keeping. It was for delivery. To them. There were several blankets on the ground in front of us. We were told to put our hidden valuables on the blankets—gold on one, silver on another, watches on a third, and so on. The prisoners who sorted these things were called "Mexico"—don't ask me why.[65] I threw in my father's silver cigarette case. When I remembered that the cigarette case held pictures of Dorka, it occurred to me that I should retrieve the pictures. Fortunately, I thought better of it. I wouldn't be telling this story if I had gone back and tried to pick the case off the pile.

The women went first into the sauna building—a large shower which could hold about fifty people. When I noticed the glass louvers in the windows, I thought, "Gee, it can't be gas, the panels are open." I didn't even know that gas chambers existed. I didn't understand exactly what the selection process had been all about. Not consciously. Yet somehow, perhaps from rumors in the ghetto, this idea had seeped into my head. We stood there for over an hour, waiting for all the women to get showered. When the women emerged, they waved to us from across a field. Everyone was waving. One woman was hollering at her husband. He couldn't pick her

---

[65] "Mexico" referred to "the third sector of Birkenau." Gutman and Berenbaum, *Anatomy of the Auschwitz Death Camp*, 395 and 553.

out. The women's heads had been shaved, and it totally changed their looks. He shouted back, "I can't see you. Raise your leg." That way he would notice her. Then we went in. We could only take our belts and shoes. We had to leave our clothes behind to be fumigated for lice and searched for valuables by the "Mexico" workers. On the way into the shower, one guy cut his foot on a piece of glass. They pulled him out and took him away. An injured foot didn't make for a good worker. Ever since, when I see broken glass on the beach, I pick it up. It's like a compulsion.

The sauna kapo, the man in charge of the shower room, was a Jewish criminal prisoner called Moise Hasid. He was the only Jew I ever encountered in the camps who had some authority, except for in camps where all the prisoners were Jews. He was six feet tall, two hundred fifty pounds, and with a few blows could kill you. As we walked to the sauna, he was holding up my riding boots and asking, "Who's shoes are these? A Sonder's?" I didn't say anything. Like with the pictures in the cigarette case, somehow I knew not to draw attention to myself. That was smart. These functionaries—I call them "middle-management" prisoners—the ones who took orders from the Germans and kept the camp functioning—would beat anyone who had pretension, like, for example, a ghetto policeman with fancy boots. I've read that when the Jews from Salonika arrived at the Auschwitz train platform, the German criminal prisoner who ran the "Canada" work detail pushed a big Greek longshoreman. The longshoreman pushed back, and the "Canada" guys beat him to death. From the moment you arrived, they wanted you to know who was boss. And it was more than that. In the camps, it was not good to be recognized as a policeman from the ghetto. Experienced prisoners often resented the ghetto police. They had relatives who died in the ghetto, and they held us responsible. The head of Rumkowski's police arrived at Auschwitz in full uniform, and Jewish prisoners killed him on the spot. Fortunately, when our transport of policemen and firemen left Łódź, we had known enough not to wear our uniforms.

I passed Moise Hasid and stepped inside, into a long hallway leading to the shower. Five or ten barbers were in the hallway, waiting to shave us from head to toe. This was to prevent lice, and, of course, the women's long hair was sent to Germany to fill mattresses. I asked the guy who shaved me if he knew anyone from Łódź, maybe Wowcio Hoyker or Szaja Bucik, somebody from the Jewish underworld who had known my father, somebody who could help me. No such luck. My father's coattails, like my hair, had been cut off.

We were inspected up and down, inside and out, in case we were still hiding valuables. Then came the shower. The water was decent, not too cold. There was a hunchback—a German Jew named Fritz. He was a nice guy. I knew him in the ghetto. He was on the transport with his father. When they got off the train, Fritz could hide his deformity under his coat and avoid selection for the gas chamber, but not when he was naked. An SS man pointed him out, and four or five "Canada" guys chased him out of the shower. He didn't want to go. He understood what it meant. They chased him like a wild animal. It was awful.

When the water went off, they chased all of us. We hustled out, dripping wet, and the "Canada" guys threw someone else's clothes at us. This wasn't exactly like going to the dry cleaners. Everyone got a shirt, pants, jacket, cap, and some ragged pieces of cloth knit together that passed for socks. In the ghetto, I could afford nice clothing, and I liked beltless slacks. That's what I wore on the transport. Now, I ended up with pants that were way too wide for me, and I didn't have a belt to hold them together. The "Canada" workers in striped uniforms were still yelling at us. Go there! Stand here! Hurry up! Hurry! I still didn't entirely comprehend the situation. If you didn't move quickly, you got hit. We were all pushing and shoving. We were terrified. Yet some prisoners were playing volleyball. I saw them when we exited the shower.

You have to understand, "Auschwitz" was a very big place. Three places, actually. Auschwitz I, the original Auschwitz, had a crematorium, but was not an extermination camp. Some prisoners lived in Auschwitz I for five years, from the beginning of the war to the end. There were reasonable barracks with bunks. The prisoners had to work, of course, but with the right job—preferably something indoors—you had a chance to survive. Auschwitz II, or Birkenau, was the extermination camp, with gas chambers and crematoria. That's where the Germans sent transports for immediate elimination. Tens of thousands were gassed on arrival. Some laborers were still needed, however. Birkenau prisoners sorted clothing, cleaned blockhouses, ran the crematoria—the important work of maintaining an extermination camp. Auschwitz III was officially called Monowitz, but was known as Buna. The prisoners slaved in a factory, trying to produce *buna*, or synthetic rubber, for I.G. Farben. The factory never really produced anything.[66] It functioned mainly to keep some German officers employed away from the Russian front. Monowitz was the worst place of the three to be a prisoner. Worse than the extermination camp. The kapos were meaner, the work harder, the terror greater. When my cousin Chaim was transferred there, one of the middle-management Jews said to him, "What do you think—we're going to pamper you like at Birkenau?" I was at Birkenau. I guess I was pampered.

The Germans generally stayed outside and let the prisoners run the camps. In Auschwitz, the top one percent, the aristocracy, were German prisoners. Mostly they were criminal prisoners. The middle management were mostly Polish prisoners who had arrived before 1943. If you had survived that long, if your camp number was only three or four digits, you were respected. You had connections. If your number was under fifty thousand, clearly you knew how to survive. We called the criminal prisoners "*zielone*"—the "green ones" or "greeners"—because they had a green triangle on their uniforms. Like in the ghetto, there were different levels of privilege among prisoners in the camps, only now I was closer to the bottom than to the top. Jews, with their red and yellow Star of David, were at the bottom of the pecking order. Only Gypsies were lower. I was a Jew with no connections, just a cut foot away from the gas chamber. No one at Auschwitz cared that I was the son of Councilman Piotr Chari. A very few Jews at Auschwitz got promoted to non-productive duty, like cleaning the latrine or ladling out soup. But Jews didn't get to play volleyball. The guys I saw playing were Poles who worked in the hospital and storage room and things like that—not pick-and-shovel laborers. They could play after quitting time. They also had a soccer field. Well, there was one Jew who got to play. When we came out of the shower, this Sonder—I think his name was Seinfeldt—asked the volleyball players if he could join their game. They let him, and he was quite good. They liked him so much, they told him to stop playing. They gave him some bread and told him, "Save your energy. You're going to need it." I heard his sister made it, but he didn't.

Like I said, I still didn't understand what I was facing. My main thought was, "I want to get out of here." I was tired. I was wearing unfamiliar clothes and holding up my new pants with my hands. I had no interest in

[66] Monowitz, or Wonowice, the largest satellite camp of Auschwitz, was "an abysmal failure in terms of output and efficiency." Gutman and Berenbaum, *Anatomy of the Auschwitz Death Camp*, 18.

watching volleyball or whatever it was we were supposed to be doing. I was wishing we could just go to the camp now and lie down, get some peace and quiet. I imagined there being a military barrack, with everyone getting a bunk. It wasn't exactly like that. When we finally got to Block 17—our new housing accommodations—it was a horse stable with a cement floor. This is where I learned my first lesson at Auschwitz: if you get hit, don't fall down, or else you'll get some more. We crowded in—there were about seven hundred in our block—and a veteran prisoner started shouting at us in Yiddish. He was very eloquent and very good at scaring people. This was his job—to greet new arrivals with threats. Corpses had been hanging from the ceiling beams the day before, he warned, corpses of prisoners who didn't obey orders. Then he demanded we give up the money and jewelry we still had hidden—in our anuses or shoes or wherever. "Give up everything," he said. "We're going to x-ray you." Some gave things up. Some didn't.

Then the *blokowy*—the block leader—a Polish political prisoner named Mietek, took over. On one end of the stable was an oven, and the heat traveled through an exhaust pipe that ran down the middle of the floor to a chimney at the other end. Mietek told all the new prisoners to stand on one side of the heating pipe. Then he ordered all the ghetto policemen to step back across to the other side. Only ten or fifteen guys stepped out. I was one of them. Stupid me. The Jewish prisoners who worked for the block leader were going to put us in our place, make sure we realized we no longer had any special status or authority. It was part of the constant intimidation to keep you scared and obedient. They began hitting us, and a few policemen fell down, which was a mistake. When you're down and showing weakness, they hit you even more. Also, they can't reach you with their fists, so they kick you or beat you with sticks. While the block leader's helpers went up and down the row, hitting and kicking policemen, I managed to escape. I took one or two slaps in the face, and that was enough for me. I took off my shoes and, holding up my pants, hurried over to where the block leader was standing. "These aren't my shoes," I explained, pretending this was the reason I had stepped forward. "I got them in the sauna. I don't know if they contain valuables or not." He told me to bend the shoes, test the flexibility of the soles, so he could see if anything was sewn inside them. When he was satisfied that they were clean, I said, "Thank you," put on my shoes, and rejoined the group, walking back on the safe side of the heating pipe to avoid the beating. By Auschwitz standards, the policemen were receiving a very mild beating—they weren't being beaten half to death—but I was happy to escape it.

There was a corollary to the "don't fall down" lesson. If you want to survive in the camps, you've got to think on your feet. You've got to understand the situation, make an instant decision, and act on it. Don't worry if the decision is right or wrong, just go with it. You didn't have to be a genius, you just had to be able to act. Call it street smarts. Call it instinct. If you had the right instinct, if you were smart, most likely you still wouldn't survive. If you didn't have it, though, you had zero chance. And zero ain't good. For a long time after the war, it bothered me any time I couldn't make an instant decision. I evaluated others similarly. I would look at a guy and think, "Gosh, he wouldn't have lasted three days." It's not something you could learn once you got to a camp. There wasn't time. Either you had it or you didn't.

I still believe the block leader knew I belonged with the Sonders getting hit. Maybe he figured that if I was smart enough to get out of it, he wouldn't interfere. Mietek was a decent guy. I never saw him hit anyone. Yes, he was in charge, and he made sure his helpers kept us terrorized, otherwise the SS wouldn't let him be the block leader. But he wasn't cruel. He didn't act like he had life-or-death power over seven hundred men. He could have been much worse. Other block leaders would beat you half to death, or all the way. Mietek would make fun of you or have someone carry you to the fence and drop you. He kept order, he did his job, but he wasn't mean. As block leader, he kept some of the valuables taken from prisoners—it was all supposed to go to the Germans—and he used them to buy vodka from SS men. His helpers warned us to stay out of his way when he was drinking, but I never saw him in a drunken rage. He'd sleep it off and that was the end of it. If I had met him after the war, I would have thanked him for having remained a human being under those conditions. I mean, the guy could have sent me back across the pipe for a beating.

As block leader, Mietek had his own little room, about four by eight feet, with a bed and a small stove. He also had ten or twelve veteran prisoners who worked for him. When they weren't beating up new arrivals, they did the everyday chores in the block—cleaning, distributing food, things like that. They slept on the floor, stretched out on about twenty feet of floor between Mietek's room and the rest of us. Although they didn't have beds, theirs was a good job. They weren't standing out in the cold. Maybe they got a little extra food, maybe soup from the bottom of the container. I'll tell you how it worked. There were two Sonders in our group who were boxers before the war. Wdowinski was a light middleweight and Fagot was a bantamweight. From our block, you could look across the wire to Camp D, and Fagot spotted a Polish prisoner who had been a European amateur champion or something like that.

"Hey, Czortek, remember me? You beat me in a fight."

"Sure, I remember you," Czortek called back across the fence.

"I'm here with Wdowinski. Is there any way you can help us?"

Being a Polish political prisoner, Czortek had some influence. He called Mietek over to the fence and told him to take care of his friends. The two Jewish boxers had found a connection. They joined Mietek's crew of helpers.

When I returned many years later, I saw the old foundations for the block where we slept. It was even smaller than I had remembered. Imagine a space suitable for, at most, fifty horses. The first fifth of the space, nearest the entrance, was reserved for a dozen guys—Mietek in his room, his helpers on the floor. The remainder of the space was the sleeping area for the rest of us. Room for forty horses or, if you prefer, seven hundred underfed men. Impossible. How could you even lie down? Very carefully. The first guy sat near the wall and spread his legs wide. The next guy sat between the first guy's legs, spread his own legs wide for the third guy, and so on, until there was a group of guys lined up. I don't remember if it was five or seven to a bunch. Then the block leader ordered them to lean back and lie to one side. That's how we slept, crammed together on the concrete floor. When you're as tired as we were, you can sleep like that. At night, you couldn't leave the building. You could barely move. In the middle of the night, someone would shift, and all five or seven would turn to the other side. If you had to relieve yourself in the bucket, you did the best you could to untangle yourself from the others. If the bucket was full, you had to wake up one of Mietek's helpers, who would assign a prisoner to empty it outside in the latrine. I never was chosen.

The first morning, as we stood outside for roll call, Mietek and his helpers started again. "Those of you who were in the police step forward." This time, nobody volunteered. So they grabbed guys at random.

"You were a policeman," the helpers insisted.

"No, not me."

"Who was?"

The correct answer was "I don't know." Then they let you go. If you raised your arm to point, or if you even started to name someone, they hit you. You didn't get a chance to finish the accusation. This was Auschwitz lesson number two, even more important than lesson one: don't snitch. Snitching won't save you, and it will only get someone else in trouble too, so don't do it. Snitches will be killed.

That was my introduction to the camps, my first twenty-four hours at Auschwitz. Getting yelled at. Getting hit. Constant terror. My privileged life in the ghetto—with my own room, and Grandmother cooking my special rations, and girlfriends, and cigarettes—was long gone. People ask what I thought at the time, what it was like to end up in Auschwitz. Was I thinking, "How can this be happening to me?" No, there wasn't much time for philosophizing. You were too busy obeying orders. I can remember only a few thoughts. I saw Mietek with the substitute coffee he made on his stove, and I realized, "I'll never again have a nice hot cup of real coffee or tea." The second or third night, sleeping in the row of guys, I had a nocturnal emission. I thought, "Gee, that will be the last time I ever do that." I saw Sergeant G., and he reminded me of his plan to hide in the cellar back in the ghetto. "Aren't you sorry you said no?" he asked. I was. Birkenau didn't seem like a place where you lasted very long.

Did I know there were gas chambers? Yes, no, and maybe. Don't look for rhyme and reason in my thinking. I knew and I didn't. That's how I kept some hope. Obviously, I knew, because I was concerned about the ventilation windows of the sauna. But when I saw fire coming out the chimneys of the crematoria, I asked Mietek what it was. He told me it was a bakery, and I believed him. I think now that he was trying not to frighten me. My cousin Chaim was in the adjoining camp, and his block leader was not so kind. He told Chaim, "*Żydki idą do nieba*"—Jews are going into the sky.

Mostly, though, I thought about food and water. We didn't get enough of either, and it dominated my thoughts. How am I going to get something to drink? What will be in the midday soup? There were no long-range thoughts, no planning, just how to supply your most basic needs from minute to minute. In the morning, standing at roll call, we got a bowl of warm, brown water, and called it "coffee." It was five guys to a bowl. We were lined up five deep, and the first in line took the first drink and passed it back. Before the first guy even swallowed, the guy in the back would shout, "Don't drink so much. I'm back here too!" So another thing I worried about was, "Where am I going to stand?" If a middle-management prisoner felt like hitting someone, he would pick someone in easy reach, like in the front row. The back row was no good either, because you might not get any substitute coffee, which was all we got for breakfast. It was safest to be in the middle of the pack. Lunch was rutabaga soup for two. Always one bowl of soup for two prisoners. And no utensil. You took a sip, then the other guy took a sip. "Don't drink so much!" It's pretty hard to divide it evenly when both of you are real hungry. If there were any pieces of potato or vegetable at the bottom of the bowl, you picked them out with your fingers. For dinner you'd get maybe a quarter pound of moldy bread with some jam or artificial honey. Birkenau was known for its moldy bread. And lack of water. There was no water available to us. No washrooms, no drinking fountain. I was thirsty all the time. And hungry. And tired. There was one other thought. There was now no doubt in my mind that my father was dead. He couldn't have survived the past five years in a place like this.

For two or three weeks, we were in camp doing nothing. They didn't gas us and they weren't putting us to work. After being counted at morning roll call, we just stood outside, rain or shine. We huddled together in groups of twenty to forty, and everybody wanted to be on the inside. It was warmer inside the huddle, and you were less likely to be hit. Once in a while, someone might come along with a bucket of water and toss it on the group. It didn't do us much good. We stood there thirsty, hungry, and tired. We weren't allowed inside the block during the day, and it wasn't safe to be sitting down. You could walk over to the sick bay, and maybe the prisoners working there would give you an aspirin. If you were really bad, or had a connection, they might send you to the hospital. Back in the ghetto, when I had climbed into the cattle car, which was pretty high off the ground, I scraped my shin. It didn't heal until after the war. I was too malnourished to heal. At Auschwitz, I would go to the sick bay and have them put a paper bandage on the wound. I took off the paper, found some dried grass, and rolled a cigarette. It was something to smoke, anyway. I can't remember how I lit it. You could also go to the latrine. There you could sit down, at least until the Jewish latrine workers chased you out. In the ghetto, latrine work was practically a death sentence, but in Auschwitz this profession had certain benefits, although it was below the Polish prisoners. Latrine workers were under a roof, protected from the elements, and no one could measure your proficiency. If you were a ditch digger, you were out in the cold, and a foreman or SS officer could easily tell how much you had dug. In the latrine, you swept with a broom and pretended to be busy. But my group didn't have jobs. We just stood there.

After two or three days, I struck it rich. I found a piece of wire that I could use as a belt around my big pants. That was a major event. Then my cousin Chaim spotted me. Birkenau was actually several camps, each containing maybe twenty-five to thirty blocks. I was in the "Gypsy Camp." The Gypsies had all been gassed to make room for Hungarian Jews, but the name remained.[67] Chaim was in the adjoining camp—Camp D—and when he saw me across the barbed wire, he threw over a bent aluminum strip. A makeshift spoon! I was the rich kid on the block. Now it was easy to divide the soup. I took a spoonful, the other guy took a spoonful, and we didn't have to use our fingers for the solids. I was less successful with my shoes. The shoes I wore to Auschwitz were stylish, like ballroom shoes. I wanted to trade them to a middle-management prisoner for a piece of bread and some wooden shoes. But my shoes were no good for marching around, so no one with access to wooden shoes wanted to trade.

Later, after I'd been in a really bad camp, I realized that my stay at Birkenau was R and R—rest and recreation. I was just there in transit, waiting to be sent to a work assignment. We didn't know this at the time. Nobody told us anything. However, that's the reason I never got a number at Auschwitz, never got a tattoo, never got the striped uniform worn by those assigned to work there. One day, after two or three weeks, the block leader called off a list of names, including mine, and sent us to Block 22, where we joined a group now totaling five hundred prisoners. Again, they didn't tell us what was going on. Two days later, they marched us to a small shower. As we were filing into the narrow entryway, a Hungarian Jew, a kapo, was walking along the main road with four or five other guys. He started yelling at us, "Quick! Quick! Quick! Get in! Get in!" Being a kapo meant he had an armband and an official assignment, a specific function. I don't know what this guy's function was. It didn't have anything to do with five hundred guys squeezing into a small shower. I guess he just wanted to show how tough he was, impress his friends or something. Why else would he hit me with a wooden bat? He hit me in the shoulder. Not real serious by Auschwitz standards. The skin that covers the bone became inflamed, though, and my shoulder bothered me for two or three weeks. After the shower, we marched out of camp to the train station, passing between the

---

[67] On August 2, 1944, the SS selected out 1,400 Gypsies for work and gassed nearly 3,000 others, effectively liquidating the Gypsy camp, which was Camp E. Gutman and Berenbaum, *Anatomy of the Auschwitz Death Camp*, 449.

men's camp and the women's camp. It was past curfew, but a door was open and a woman inside a block yelled my name and waved. I waved back, but I didn't recognize her. See, it was hard to recognize people when they were emaciated and worn out. In the ghetto, we called it *klepsydra*, but in the camps it was *Musselman*—don't ask me why.[68] Since this woman recognized me, you can tell that I still had some vitality, I wasn't *Musselman*. I had arrived at Auschwitz in decent condition, not totally malnourished like the less privileged from Łódź. I wasn't among the worst off. I had a chance to make it. It still nags at me—who was that emaciated woman who knew me? I doubt she could have made it. I'll never know.

I waved to her, and then I said goodbye to Auschwitz. They didn't tell us that we were leaving. They didn't tell us where we were going. They just marched five hundred of us from the block to the shower and then straight to the train. We sat on the train for some hours before leaving, then traveled west into Germany. The train trip was about one third as long as the trip from Łódź. We arrived in the morning in the small town of Wüstegiersdorf in Silesia.[69] We were headed for the Gross-Rosen concentration camp, but we didn't go to the main camp. Instead, from the train station, we walked for an hour or so to the Kaltwasser work camp, a satellite camp of Gross-Rosen. It was a sunny day. Probably September. Behind the barbed wire fence, we could see wooden buildings with glass windows. Some of the buildings weren't finished. The camp was brand new, and we were its first lucky residents. Outside the camp, SS men had barracks and guard booths. Inside the camp, medical personnel waited to process us. We marched through camp and were assigned to a block. We received a shot—fifty guys to one needle—can you imagine? Well, it wasn't *our* health they were concerned about. When we went to work, there might be some contact with the local civilian population, and the SS wanted to prevent the spread of disease into the area.

Before our group had departed Auschwitz, the Germans had appointed one of us to be *Lagerälteste*, the "camp elder" or head prisoner. Now, in our new camp, the *Lagerälteste*, a Polish Jew who had been in Auschwitz since 1943, made a reception speech. He told us there were only Jews inside the fence, he was in charge, and it was going to be a good camp. No beatings. He didn't know where we'd be sent to work every day. That wasn't his

---

[68] *Musselman* means Muslim.
[69] Wüstegiersdorf, Germany, is now Głuszyca, Poland.

responsibility. In camp, though, he wouldn't add to our suffering. He kept his word, by the way, and was never prosecuted for collaborating with the Nazi regime. After the speech, he selected guys for internal camp work. He appointed two leaders per block and two or three camp policemen. He also chose guys for kitchen duty, a very desirable assignment. You had to have an "in" with him to get chosen. Then we sat around doing nothing for two or three weeks. Time for my bruised shoulder to stop hurting. We were being quarantined in case we were carrying some disease. But this was just temporary. We were no longer in transit. We each got a prisoner number. I was 17596. We were in Kaltwasser to work for the Reich.

4

GROSS-ROSEN

Work camps were not meant for survival. If you followed the rules, if you worked as hard as the Germans demanded and ate as little as they allotted, you wouldn't make it. To survive, you needed three things. The first I already mentioned. You had to have smarts, which meant knowing when to take initiative and when to avoid drawing attention. I'm not saying I survived because I'm so clever. By itself, being smart wasn't enough. You also had to have help. Being a loner wasn't a good idea. You needed friends among the prisoners, guys who might share a little food or look out for you, maybe give you a break in your work assignment. You also needed an act of kindness here and there from a privileged prisoner or a German supervisor, like being assigned to an easier work group. Still, with help and smarts, the odds were against you. The third thing you needed was luck. You can call it what you want—God's will or whatever. There were moments when things could have gone one way or the other, you got selected or you didn't, you were sent here and not there, and there's no reasonable explanation. Just luck.

I had already had lots of luck. I was lucky that I chose to stay in the Łódź ghetto and not go to Warsaw with my mother. At that moment, who could have known that the chance of survival was better in Łódź? I was lucky that my stepmother tricked me into going to school in the ghetto. Why did she want me to continue school? She didn't know that graduating from Rumkowski Gymnasium would allow me to become a Sonder and, thus, stay healthy enough to survive ghetto conditions and escape the initial selection at

Auschwitz. I was lucky that my aunt went to Rumkowski when I was in the hospital. Even with my father's coattails, I needed that luck. And when the coattails were severed, when I became just another prisoner on a transport of five hundred sent from Auschwitz to work at Gross-Rosen, I would need luck more than ever. The Germans' plan was to work us to death, and it wouldn't take long. I'm lucky to be alive today, telling my story.

Recently, when another survivor heard I'd been at Gross-Rosen, he said, "That was a tough camp." It's true. Gross-Rosen was one of the worst. Other tough camps were Mauthausen, Flossenbürg, and Natzweiler-Struthof. By comparison, Auschwitz-Birkenau, though an extermination camp, wasn't a tough camp for the prisoners who worked there. Not by the standards of the time. Tough camps had stone quarries where prisoners dropped dead from exhaustion. Other characteristics of a tough camp included middle-management prisoners who were extra selfish, keeping more food for themselves, and a German commandant who was especially mean. One prisoner at Gross-Rosen organized a warm jacket—a great treasure—but he couldn't wear it because it didn't have the correct camp markings painted on the back. He hid the jacket under his mattress, hoping to organize some paint for the markings. We heard this story at Kaltwasser. The Germans found the jacket and accused him of preparing to escape. He had a civilian jacket in his possession, after all. He had been so happy when he got the jacket, and now it got him killed. The German commandant forced the guy's own father to hang him. That's what happened at a tough camp.

Kaltwasser was a satellite camp, or sub-camp, administered by German officials at the main camp of Gross-Rosen, perhaps twenty miles away. The camp commandant at Kaltwasser—the *Lagerführer*—was a low-ranking noncommissioned SS officer, like a staff sergeant. His deputy commandant—the *Unterlagerführer*—was the equivalent of a corporal. Their function was mainly to count the prisoners and make sure we went to work. The officials at the main camp took away sick prisoners, sent other prisoners to replace them, gave orders to the SS guard details, and so on. At Kaltwasser, there was a small infirmary for sick prisoners. One day during our period of quarantine, a high-ranking SS officer from Auschwitz came for inspection. The officer was a physician and very likely was Mengele.[70] He

---

[70] Josef Mengele was an SS officer and a physician at Birkenau who used prisoners for human experiments. Gutman and Berenbaum, *Anatomy of the Auschwitz Death Camp*, 319-328.

ordered the thirty or so sick prisoners sent back to Auschwitz, to Birkenau, to be gassed and cremated. Their transport left about a week later and included a prisoner named Kaufman. He had been the fire chief in the ghetto, a real big shot who had worked closely with the Germans.[71] When we came through Auschwitz, he got stuck with wooden shoes. I don't know for sure, but I suspect he arrived at Auschwitz in full fire brigade uniform or at least wearing fancy riding boots. That was the type of guy he was. The boots, of course, would have been confiscated on arrival. Whether my suspicion is right or not, the wooden shoes killed him. You couldn't walk in wooden shoes. You would get sores where the outside of your foot rubbed against the wood, and they only got worse. Without adequate protein and vitamin C, open wounds won't heal. Kaufman's feet were so badly swollen from infection that he could hardly walk. I guess when he left Kaltwasser, he knew he was going back to Birkenau. He said, "I've gone through lots of fires, I'll go through one more." And to think that at Auschwitz I had been trying to trade my shoes for wooden ones and a little bread.

There were maybe forty boys around age twelve to fourteen in Kaltwasser, and they went on the same transport. The same high-ranking inspector from Auschwitz announced that all the children would go to another camp because the work at Kaltwasser would be too hard for them. The boys were all placed in one room, and an adult prisoner was assigned to make sure they didn't escape and blend in with the other prisoners. Not that the boys wanted to. They got better food in their room—milk soup or something—and they were going someplace better, someplace easier. I know one survivor, Josl B., who managed to escape the boys' room. The other boys, of course, went back to Birkenau.

For the rest of us, sitting in quarantine, we were sort of at leisure. There wasn't much work in the camp. We dug a pool to hold water, supposedly in case the camp waterworks were bombed, and that was about it. The *Lagerführer* ordered us to do calisthenics. He asked who could lead the group, and one prisoner volunteered. That wasn't smart. Maybe he thought he would be rewarded. Think about it, though. In the middle of several hundred guys, you could loaf and cheat and not do all the squats and jumping jacks. When you're malnourished, it's critical to conserve as much strength as possible. Out in front, the leader had to keep going for the whole hour or

---

[71] Henryk Kaufman was the head of the ghetto fire department. Dobroszycki, *The Chronicle*, 24 and 500.

however long we had to exercise. The *Lagerälteste*—the head prisoner—asked if there were any singers or dancers in the group, and seven or eight guys came forward. This proved to be a good move for them, as it later led to a slightly privileged position. One of the volunteers was Lolek C., my friend from grade school and from the gymnasium and gasworks in the ghetto. Lolek had a terrific singing voice. He and some other guys, mostly Sonders, had performed in a vaudeville review in the ghetto.[72] I never saw it. Tickets were only for the super-privileged. Now the *Lagerälteste* told them to prepare some entertainment for our group as we sat in quarantine.

After a week or so, I volunteered to dig *kopce*—trenches for storing potatoes and vegetables. The work was out behind the kitchen, about twenty or thirty feet beyond the fence. We filled the trenches with potatoes and kept piling them on, creating a long row of piled potatoes. Then we covered it with dirt and straw. Eventually, heavy snow would cover the row and protect the potatoes from frost. We were storing food for the winter even though the Russians were closing in. Like many things in the camps, it made no sense, but never mind. I didn't volunteer because I was calculating the future. I volunteered so I could organize some potatoes for right then. That's how I got the biggest scare of my young life. After my first day of work, I re-entered the camp through a small gate near the kitchen and ran between barracks to avoid the SS guards on the main road. They occasionally walked through camp to make their presence felt. I was heading for the back door of my building. I was three quarters of the way down the path—I had almost made it—when the *Unterlagerführer* spotted another prisoner taking the same route. He called the prisoner out, and then he saw me. The *Unterlagerführer* was tall and thin, like a match, like an underfed basketball player, and he was tough. He was known to beat up people. He superficially searched the first prisoner, patted him down, found nothing. Then he turned to me. Anywhere he would have touched me he would have found potatoes. I was loaded with them—in my pants, in my jacket, in my sleeves. He just said, "*Kannst laufen.*" I can still hear the words. "You can go." Perhaps I was too dirty, or he didn't want to bother bending down. Either way, I'm not complaining about my luck. I shared the potatoes with two Sonders who slept between me and the wall. We had no way to cut or cook the potatoes, so we ate them like apples.

---

[72] Dobroszycki, *The Chronicle*, 57, describes a revue "composed of skits, genre pieces touching on current events, monologues, and dance performances."

When I first walked in with the organized potatoes, my friends asked, "Chari, what happened? You're white like the wall."

"I don't want potatoes," I told them. "I don't want that work no more." I was totally scared. The guards had forced one prisoner to stand at the gate all night with his genitals exposed and a potato in his mouth. He had been caught with a single potato. Had he found my load of potatoes, the tall SS man might have beaten me to death right there. That wasn't the scariest moment of the war for me, but it was close. Naturally, it was about food. Little else mattered.

Even with moments like that, at Kaltwasser we didn't experience the constant terror like we had at Auschwitz, at least not in camp. Yes, we were sleeping on wooden floors and there wasn't enough to eat. Yes, there was always the chance we would get sent to back Birkenau. But for the moment, we weren't there in the shadow of the chimneys. And there were no greeners—non-Jewish prisoners—yelling at us and pushing us around. Kapos didn't come by and hit us for no good reason. Sleeping conditions were a little better too. The blocks weren't quite as crowded as at Birkenau. There was straw on the floor, and everyone had a blanket. We even had the song-and-dance show a few times. We were lucky to be at a sub-camp rather than the Gross-Rosen main camp. It wasn't R and R, though, not after the quarantine period was over and we went to work. That's when the vaudeville ended and the real suffering began.

The Germans were building some kind of dream city, maybe to hide the top brass, in the mountains near Kaltwasser. To be more specific, several private companies under German government contract were in charge of construction, and they paid the SS for our labor. Organization Todt, the most important of the companies, was like a corps of engineers, with a military structure and officer rankings, but it wasn't part of the German army. The project was mostly in bunkers four or five stories underground. As soon as a bunker was finished, they planted some trees over it. One time, walking to work, I saw a hill open up and four guys walk out. Then it closed up and you couldn't see anything, not even the door. The area was full of installations like that. The underground work was top secret and done by Italian POWs and German civilians. We never went down there. They used us above ground to dig drainage ditches, break stones in the quarry, carry steel rails for a narrow gauge train track, and mix cement. It was backbreaking work, especially if you were already tired and malnourished. The block leaders woke us up at five o'clock in the morning—"Up, up, up!

Out, out, out!"—to stand at roll call in the dark, enjoying the bitter cold. One time an SS man pointed to the moon rising over the mountains and said something like, "Isn't it nice? If it wasn't for us, you would never get to see it." They counted us, we got the usual brown water known as "coffee," and we stood there for over an hour. Stood there doing nothing, except freezing. After that cold start, we marched for an hour and a half uphill to the work site. We worked all day, with a thirty-minute break for the midday soup. During the break, you could take a quick nap. When it was too dark to work any longer, we walked for an hour downhill to camp for the evening soup. There weren't enough bowls to go around, so only one block could eat at a time. By the time everyone ate and could go to sleep, it was ten o'clock or later. Then up at five again to see the moon. After a few weeks of this exhausting routine without proper nourishment, guys started dying on the job, maybe one or two a day. There are three things you can never get used to: lack of sleep, hunger, and being cold.

The food at Kaltwasser, what there was of it, wasn't entirely terrible. The midday soup could be something good, like milk soup with macaroni. It could also be inedible, made from dried onion skins, the equivalent of sawdust. Like my grandfather said, "You pour away the liquid, then toss aside the solids." With the evening soup, we received bread and *zulage*, which means "in addition to." Bread plus. The bread was typically four slices, about half a pound. The *zulage* was different from day to day. It could be a bit of marmalade or artificial honey, which was just some melted sugar. It could be a pat of butter and some Camembert cheese. On better days, it was a piece of sausage and some margarine. The bread and *zulage* were meant to be saved for breakfast, but everybody ate it right away. There was a big guy, a blacksmith, who was very strong and handy with a hammer. The Germans made him break up large stones in the quarry, and he thought he needed more bread to maintain his strength. Somehow, without knowing anything about nutrition, I understood that what a prisoner needed most was more protein. The blacksmith and I struck a deal. I always gave him half my bread, and he would give me his *zulage*, no matter what it was. I wanted the extra cheese and sausage for protein, even if some days I only got some marmalade. At the going rate of exchange in the camp—bread for cheese or marmalade or whatever—the big blacksmith probably came out slightly ahead. However, what he gained in carbohydrates he lost in protein, and it probably cost him. The Germans eventually worked him to death.

Our work was supervised by German civilians, but we belonged to the SS. The SS personnel at Kaltwasser weren't trained as concentration camp guards. They weren't the super-sadists you read about. A group of about twenty-five SS men escorted us up and down the mountain and observed us at work, and there was a good group and a bad group. They alternated days. The SS men in the good group were young soldiers, perhaps around age twenty-five, from the Waffen SS. They had been wounded while fighting the Russians on the eastern front. No longer useful on the battlefield, they were transferred to camp duty, and they were halfway decent to us. They treated us like we were almost human. The good group was on duty one day when a civilian supervisor hit a prisoner. An SS corporal grabbed the civilian by the crotch and told him, "These are my prisoners. If there's a problem, you tell me and I'll take care of it. But don't you touch them. They're my responsibility. Your responsibility is to get the work completed." After that, no one touched us when he was on duty. Another guard in the good group would leave part of his breakfast in a crumpled newspaper so that a prisoner would find it. A little extra bread for one guy didn't compensate for all the suffering, but at least these guards weren't cruel. The guards in the bad group were younger, perhaps around eighteen years old, and meaner. They weren't old enough to have been combat veterans. Their training, I suspect, was in the Hitler Youth, where they were taught that anyone in a concentration camp deserved what he got. That's just my speculation. With those teenagers on duty, we were constantly facing some kind of harassment. We always felt scared. I remember one young guard stabbed the point of his bayonet in a prisoner's back end for not walking fast enough up the hill.

Then there were the kapos. A kapo was the prisoner in charge of a work group, or *kommando*. His job was to yell and scream and beat the prisoners in his *kommando* to satisfy the Germans that they were giving maximum effort. When the quarantine ended, the *Lagerälteste* chose the entertainers to be kapos. I guess he was rewarding them for performing for us. Kapos didn't have to work so hard and they got an extra midday soup. Lolek got the job, but was too nice. He wouldn't scream at workers or hit them. After a week or so, he was demoted back to an ordinary prisoner. Other kapos could be pretty tough—they wanted to keep their jobs. That's how it was. Civilian supervisors to make sure you did the work right, Jewish kapos to make sure you worked without pausing, and SS guards to make sure you worked all day, every day, and didn't run away.

The first *kommando* I was in dug ditches and mixed cement. Digging ditches was difficult because anyone could easily see how much progress you were making. You couldn't loaf. When we mixed cement, maybe eight guys shoveled sand and gravel into the mixer. That was hard work, shoveling for hours, but at least the German foreman kept the mixer set at a decent speed. Two prisoners were assigned to the sacks of dry cement. They emptied sacks into a box with handles like a stretcher and carried the box ten or twenty feet to the mixer. Once enough sand and gravel were in the mixer, they dumped in the dry cement and went back for more. They had the better job, even if the box was heavy. They usually had to wait thirty seconds or so at the mixer while the other guys shoveled. That was thirty seconds of rest. Every little bit counted. We were supposed to take turns at that task, but when my turn ended I took some initiative. I asked the German foreman if I could keep hauling cement since I already knew how. I could speak German rather well, thanks to the strictest German teacher in pre-war Łódź, and that helped. Being able to communicate with people in authority was an advantage in the camps. Perhaps my German skills made me seem a little less foreign, a little more human to the foreman. He agreed to my request. Anyway, what did he care? His concern was pouring the cement properly. He was a cement specialist and a decent guy. Yes, there were decent Germans. When an officer from Organization Todt showed up for inspection, the foreman turned up the mixer speed to impress the inspector, then turned it slower as soon as the guy left. He said, "No one can work at the speed they want."

Still, I wanted to change *kommandos*. Dumping cement and digging ditches was hard work, and, with so little rest and so little food, I wasn't going to last for long. The Sonder who was next to me on the train to Auschwitz— the good-looking guy who screwed the girl—was a kapo, and one morning I asked if I could join his *kommando*. He normally had about thirty prisoners under him, and a couple guys were out sick, so he let me in. The advantage of this *kommando* was there was no set assignment. Some days you worked even harder than in the cement *kommando*. Maybe you loaded stones onto a truck or you carried steel train rails. Other days you did next to nothing, like unload potatoes. At the work site, there was a building where the German civilian workers were housed and fed. That's where the potatoes went. The cook, a young Polish woman, took a liking to our handsome kapo, and she gave him things, like a pair of gloves, some extra soup. Sometimes there were enough leftovers from the Germans' lunch for him to share with his *kommando*. Sometimes we could go into the building and warm ourselves.

You see, besides being exhausted, we were always cold, except in the crowded blocks.[73] It was now autumn, and we were poorly dressed in the clothing we got at Auschwitz. To stay warm at work, we wore cement bags under our jackets. You put a bag in front, a bag in back, and tied them together with wire over your shoulders. A cement bag is double-layered paper, so when it's empty you have four layers. That's pretty good insulation. If you didn't have cement bags, you might wrap your camp blanket under your jacket. Either way, you had to be careful. If the civilian supervisor caught you wearing cement bags at work, you were in trouble for sabotage because the bags were reusable. He would tell the SS guard, who would hit you a few times with his whip. You could, however, wear your camp blanket at work. The German supervisor didn't care. It was your blanket. But when you were walking out of camp to go to work, an SS man counted you. If he caught you wearing your blanket, he would hit you a few times and make you remove it. Taking a blanket out of camp was forbidden because you might trade it or use it to hide something. But if the SS man noticed you wearing cement bags as you entered or exited camp, he didn't care. Bags weren't camp property. Got it? We also wrapped pieces of cement bag around our feet and legs. We had socks from Auschwitz, but they were just two pieces of ragged cloth sewn together in the shape of a bowl. And when we carried railroad track, we wore those pathetic socks on our hands, otherwise our fingers would freeze to the steel.

After work, when we got back to camp, we could take a shower. It wasn't obligatory and it wasn't pleasant. The shower was always cold and crowded. There were no towels. I'm not sure about soap. Sometimes the guards would order an entire block to shower that night. Remember, hygiene in eastern Europe at that time, even before the war, was not like hygiene in the West now. We weren't used to frequent bathing. There was a saying, "You have sex once a day and shower once a week." So in the camp, bathing wasn't a major concern. But one time I woke up in the middle of the night and asked a guard if I could take a shower. Looking back, I'm not sure how I had the courage to make such an audacious request. Fortunately, the guard didn't think it was a big deal. He warned me that the water would be cold, but it was always cold, even during the day. Kaltwasser literally means cold

---

[73] For more on Kaltwasser conditions, see Wolfgang Benz and Barbara Distel, *Der Ort des Terrors: Geschichte der Nationalsozialistischen Konzentrationslager* Band 6 (München: Verlag C.H. Beck, 2007), 354-355.

water! I took a shower in the empty, quiet shower room. I could take my time. I remember it was a nice moment in a bad situation.

The situation was bad and getting worse, even with the occasional easy day at work. Prisoners were dying. It was just too much work with so little food and so much exposure to the elements. How did I feel when I saw someone drop dead? I had no response. It was just matter of fact, like today seeing someone throw away a cigarette butt. There was nothing you could do. You were only thinking about the next soup. One day during the midday break, as we sat in the mud, eating our soup or trying to nap, a prisoner walked up to an SS guard and said, "I can't take it anymore. Shoot me."

"I can't just shoot you. You have to run away. Go down that road." The prisoner went a little ways down the road. The guard raised his rifle and shouted, "Halt! Come back!" The prisoner walked back! He didn't run away. "I can't shoot you if you come back," the guard told him, "dying isn't that easy." That was the end of it.

But you see the level of desperation. I was getting close to that point myself. I was exhausted and depressed. There was a narrow gauge railroad that carried material in and out of the mountain bunkers. One day I saw a railroad engineer letting off hot water and steam, and I ran over and washed my hands in the water. He asked, "Don't you guys get any hot water?" When I said no, he let it run a little longer for me. What a decent man. I looked at the train engine and thought, "Gosh, if that was a crematorium, I'd just walk right in and I'd be warm for a second and then it would be over with."

We had been working for about two weeks, and I don't think I could have survived two more. And remember, because of my privileges in the ghetto, I was better nourished than most of the prisoners when we arrived at Kaltwasser. I was still wearing the black dress shoes I had brought from the ghetto, and I wrapped too much paper around my right foot, which put pressure on my toes and decreased the blood circulation. Back in the ghetto, in 1942, I had developed an abscess in the big toe of my right foot, probably from an ingrown toenail. A ghetto doctor removed the nail while I was under light general anesthesia, like laughing gas or something. Now, with the shoe too tight, the abscess returned. A German foreman asked, "What's the matter? You're usually such a good worker." I told him I had an abscess and shivers and high temperature and really felt awful. Fortunately, there were a few good Germans. This foreman was one of them. He said, "Put a tool in a bucket, and I'll pretend I need you and another guy to carry it for me." When the foreman went inside to eat, the other prisoner and I went with him and sat in the corner. The foreman sat at a table and peeled and ate an apple. He carved out some bacon and tossed away the rind. Again, it was helpful to know German. Very apologetically and respectfully, I asked, "Sir, could I have the bacon rind and the apple peel?" You couldn't really swallow the bacon rind—it was too hard—but you could chew on it all day. The apple peel would be a real treat.

"Yes, of course," the foreman replied, "but what are you going to do with it?"

"I'm going to eat it."

He looked at me—it was like a revelation to him.

"Share it with your friend."

"Yes, of course. Thank you."

The foreman supervised us every day at work, he could see our thin bodies and sunken eyes, and he was a kind man, yet somehow he had no idea how hungry we were. Maybe he didn't want to know, the same way I didn't want to know that people were starving in the ghetto. When we went back outside, the foreman saw to it that I didn't work too hard. Toward the end of the day, though, somebody pushed a cart over my toe and the abscess broke open. In the evening, I went to the camp physician, a Jewish prisoner from Łódź. He wasn't sympathetic.

"You can go to work like that," he insisted.

"I can't put on my shoe."

"Do the best you can."

The next morning, at roll call, I went and stood with the sick ones. There were eight prisoners reporting sick. The physician told the *Lagerführer*, "These five are sick and these three just came over here on their own. They don't want to go to work."

"Let me look at them," the *Lagerführer* replied. Of the five presented as sick, he sent four to the camp hospital and one to work. Then he looked at the other three, which included me. We weren't "officially" sick. He sent one to the hospital. He sent the second guy to work, where he died that day. Then he came to me. The *Lagerführer* was not a nice man. He always carried a whip or a stick for hitting prisoners. But he saved my life. He looked at my foot and said, "That will heal nicely. Let's put him in the hospital for a few days." Unless the camp physician happened to like you and made sure you received decent care, the camp hospital was not a good place to be. After a day or two you were rested, but you had nothing to do. You would lie there all day, with not enough to eat, just thinking about food. Fortunately for me, the *Lagerführer* changed his mind. "Wait," he said, "your hands look healthy. You can peel potatoes."

It was probably the end of September, 1944, when I went into the potato peeling business. As a potato peeler, I was aware that I was once again privileged, that I didn't have it so bad. Potato peeling was a good business to be in. First, you didn't have to stand in roll call and march up the mountain. When everybody got up at five o'clock and stood outside, I went straight to the peeling room—a small barrack where twenty-five to thirty guys worked— and started peeling potatoes and vegetables. The peeling room was about twenty feet from the kitchen, so you could easily deliver the potatoes there. When the *Lagerführer* came in for inspection, the peeling room kapo would shout, "Attention," but the *Lagerführer* would just say, "Keep working." Second, potato peelers were indoors, protected from the weather. One morning it was raining so hard you wouldn't send a dog out. There was no way you could pour cement or dig ditches. The SS guards still made the *kommandos* march up the mountain. Why? Because the SS got paid for delivering workers to the job site. If it was too wet for work, that wasn't their problem. The guys walked up the mountain and walked back, three hours in the pouring rain, so the SS could collect their money. I saw them coming back, miserable in their soaked clothing, and I cried. For some reason, I had to go into a block leader's room—maybe to deliver something. The block leader and his assistant (who I think was his brother) were there, nice and warm and dry. That's when I broke down in tears. I felt so sorry for the other prisoners walking in the rain—such a stupid, useless thing. I don't remember crying any other time in the camps.

Besides being indoors, potato peelers could lay their hands on more food. You could eat what you were peeling. You could organize an extra midday soup from the kitchen. You could organize potatoes. Someone normally inspected you when you left work in the late evening, but not when you went to the latrine during the work day, so it was easy. You hid potatoes in your clothes, went out to the latrine, and stopped by the barracks. You did this after the workers returned from the mountain—they quit work before we did—and you gave the potatoes to your friends. I had one close call. The kapo had his back turned, and I was almost out the door when he noticed me.

"Where are you going?"

"I need to use the latrine."

"Let me search you."

He had been a Sonder in the ghetto. He knew all about arm potatoes and leg potatoes. He searched me head to toe, with one exception. I was standing on steps, with one foot a step higher than the other. I was standing that way for a reason, and I guess it worked. He thoroughly searched the leg on the higher step. When he searched the leg on the lower step, he stopped at the knee. The pant leg was tied at the ankle and holding potatoes, but he didn't reach down there. If he had, I would have been marching up the hill to make cement the next morning. That was just luck. He didn't know the potatoes were there.

Potato peels were easy to hide in your clothes, and I always brought some back to the barracks to give away to other prisoners. One evening, Niutek S. proposed a trade. Niutek had been one of my best friends in the ghetto. He had been a Sonder and usually came to the get-togethers in my room. Now he was tired and beat up from working on the mountain and wanted to exchange his *zulage*, which was marmalade, for some of my potato peels. I turned him down. This might not make much sense, but I felt like I would be degrading him, or taking advantage of him, by giving him something as pathetic as potato peels for marmalade. At the Kaltwasser rate of exchange, the marmalade was worth three-fourths of a slice of bread or maybe an entire slice. The potato peels weren't really worth anything. They were just something to chew on. Of course, I should have given him potato peels for free. It's hard to convey our way of thinking and acting in those circumstances. What seems so obvious in hindsight wasn't so obvious in the camps. About ten or fifteen years ago, I was at a dinner party in Tel Aviv. The woman sitting next to me asked if I had known Adek S. in the ghetto. I hadn't, but it turned out that Adek was Niutek's older brother and the woman was their cousin. When she asked about them, I immediately thought about not giving the potato peels to Niutek. An uncomfortable feeling developed in my stomach. It was over sixty years ago that I refused Niutek's request, and I still feel guilty, even today.

Although peeling potatoes was better than mixing cement, you still had to work fast. You production could be measured. The cook was a German civilian employed by Organization Todt. He was something like a master sergeant, and he wanted the job done right. Once, when we were too slow, he went into a rage. He came in about four o'clock in the afternoon and shouted, "I need more potatoes. I don't have enough to make a good soup tonight. Your friends won't get a good soup." That was more about his pride as a cook than about the prisoners' health. He was paid to provide a nourishing meal to the labor force, and he took great pride in making something out of nothing. He would boil bones in soup two or three times, then crack them open and boil them again the next day. He also threw a tantrum when he caught a kitchen worker organizing a slab of butter. The *Lagerälteste* came running because he didn't want the cook to get the SS involved. "Don't worry," the *Lagerälteste* said. "We'll punish him. We'll teach him a lesson. He's going to get twenty-five with a stick." He took the kitchen worker to his block and had him lie over a stool. When the cook came out of the kitchen and walked toward the block, the *Lagerälteste* started hitting the stool with a stick. Every time he hit the stool, the kitchen worker would scream. That's how the *Lagerälteste* and his police ran the camp. They gave the impression of discipline, but they never beat anybody. When the cook was just outside the block, below a high window, he could hear the beating and the screams and he said, "That's enough. Let him go. That's enough." He wasn't a bad man. He just wanted everyone to get the food they were entitled to, no less and no more.

Potato peeling wasn't supposed to be a permanent career. The *Lagerführer* sent prisoners to the camp hospital or to the peeling room to recover. If they recovered, he sent them back up the mountain to work until they dropped. If a prisoner really had no hope of recovery, the *Lagerführer* sent him to the hospital at the Gross-Rosen main camp, where they threw you on the floor and let you die. Once or twice, the *Lagerführer* came into the potato shack and tested us one by one. You had to put your foot on a bench, and he pressed his finger into your ankle. If the impression remained, you had edema—water retention due to protein deficiency—and little chance of recovery. That was the selection. You were sent to the main camp hospital and that was the end of it. It's possible that sitting on a stool all day, peeling potatoes, allowed water to accumulate more readily in your legs, so even that job wasn't safe. One way or the other, you were doomed. Work to death on the mountain or peel potatoes until you get sent back up the mountain or to the main camp hospital to die.

That's why, after about a month peeling potatoes, I chose to return to the Birkenau extermination camp. Even after my toe improved, I had managed to remain a potato peeler. I still had the open wound from scraping my leg while boarding the cattle car in Łódź. When I worked on the mountain, I used a piece of paper from a cement bag to keep the wound covered. In the potato shack, I scratched the wound so it wouldn't heal, so the *Lagerführer* wouldn't send me back up the mountain. Near the end of

October, however, the *Lagerführer* announced that the Kaltwasser prisoners were moving to a camp closer to the work site. Those strong enough to march for an hour and a half up the mountain would go there and keep their same work assignments. Those too sick to march would be transferred elsewhere. The camp *schreiber*, a Czech Jew, told us that "elsewhere" was Auschwitz. The *schreiber* was the prisoner in charge of the camp secretarial work. Germans love keeping careful records—even, it turned out, in concentration camps—so we had a *schreiber*. Every morning, while the other prisoners stood at roll call, he walked to his work at the SS administration office inside the fence. As he walked, he proudly held his toothbrush for all to see. It was the only toothbrush in camp. Quite a status symbol. The *schreiber* had daily contact with the SS, and when he told us that the ones who couldn't walk to the new camp would be sent back to Auschwitz to be gassed, it made sense. We knew that the sick men and the young boys had been transported back to Auschwitz. And somehow we knew about the gas chambers. I decided I would rather die cleanly at Auschwitz than die slowly and painfully at the new camp. I didn't trust that I would still be a potato peeler, and I knew I wouldn't last long working outdoors. Some of my friends encouraged me to make the march. They would help me up the hills if my foot or shin weren't entirely healed. But I'd had enough.

The *Lagerführer* limited the number of "sick"—those unable or unwilling to climb the mountain—to 150. Approximately 500 prisoners had originally come from Auschwitz to Kaltwasser. Between 50 and 100 had been transported out or died at Kaltwasser. That means between 250 and 300 capable workers marched off to Lorchen, the new camp. According to Lolek, the *Lagerführer* told them, "You are all cheats. You were supposed to last only a few weeks, and I've been with you two months." Most of that group, including the big blacksmith and Niutek S., didn't make it. The work killed some of them. Later, when the Russians approached, the Germans evacuated the new camp, and most of the prisoners dropped from exhaustion or were shot during a death march to other camps. Lolek managed to keep himself and his father alive. They ended up in Theresienstadt, where they were liberated. As for the 150 "sick" ones—the *schreiber* was wrong. We didn't go to Birkenau. This was the start of November, 1944. The Russians were advancing from the east, and the Germans had begun the process of liquidating Auschwitz.[74] It wouldn't have been unusual if the SS had marched us into the woods and shot us. That didn't happen either. More inexplicable luck. After the unlucky "healthier" ones headed up the mountain, we walked a half hour or so, across flatlands, back to Wüstergiersdorf, where the city baths were open to us—real humane conditions, the best treatment I'd seen since Łódź. We put our clothing in a big pile for de-lousing while we took hot showers in a huge shower room. After the de-lousing, it was first come, first served. If you found a good jacket, you took it. Then we walked outside the town to a new hospital camp. The Germans were losing the war and had a manpower shortage, and yet they built a new hospital camp for Jewish prisoners. There was no logic in the camps, so don't look for it. I had volunteered for the gas chamber and ended up in a hospital bed—five new barracks, two prisoners to a bed, and physician prisoners to attend us. Not that I'm complaining.

We were still prisoners of the SS, though, and still had to navigate between cruel Germans and decent ones. The hospital camp commandant—another low-ranking noncommissioned SS officer—ordered me to bring in coal to heat our new block. I was limping, and, after I had carried two loads, another SS man noticed me. "You can barely walk," he said, and assigned the task to another prisoner. The commandant returned and saw me standing there. "I told you to carry coal," he said, and he hit me. I didn't try to explain. I didn't fall down. I had learned that lesson at Auschwitz. You take the beating and don't blame someone else. The other SS man stepped in. He didn't have to get involved, didn't have to risk an argument with his superior, but he did. He explained that I was limping and he had relieved me. That was that.

One guy who really knew how to deal with German guards was Alfred, a veteran Jewish prisoner and the head nurse at the new hospital. He was from Marseilles, where he'd been arrested for smuggling Jewish children from France into Switzerland. In 1942, he went on a transport of 1,500 prisoners from France to Auschwitz. He told me that only two prisoners from that transport were still alive. Anyone who'd been in the camps since 1942, as Alfred had, obviously knew something about survival, knew what he could

---

[74] The Germans ceased using the Auschwitz gas chambers in November, 1944, and, in December, began dismantling the crematoria. The evacuation of prisoners began on January 18, and Soviet troops arrived on January 27. Gutman and Berenbaum, *Anatomy of the Auschwitz Death Camp*, 237, 410-411.

and couldn't get away with. In Auschwitz, an SS officer had reprimanded him for not showing the proper deference.

"Don't you respect me?!" the officer asked. "Take your hands from your pockets."

"I respect someone who is older or wiser than I am," Alfred told him. "You I only fear. That's why I'll take my hands out of my pockets." The officer smacked him in the face with his whip.

Alfred told me that story, and maybe it sounds unbelievable—a Jewish prisoner at Auschwitz talking back to a German and living to tell about it— but I saw firsthand this attitude of his. In the hospital one time, an SS man came inside to warm up and immediately started yelling at the prisoners in the room, telling them what to do, deciding who could or could not go to the latrine. Alfred quickly reminded him that he was supposed to be outside, in the bitter cold, guarding the gate so prisoners didn't escape, not inside directing traffic. "Quiet down," Alfred warned him, "or I'll make sure you're sent back out there." The guard was a wounded soldier, not a hardcore SS officer, so Alfred knew he could threaten him like this.

Alfred took a liking to me—I don't know why. He'd spent two years in medical school in France and two more years studying theology. I was just a ghetto policeman from Łódź. Maybe part of it was that I could communicate with him in German. Again, I'm not complaining. Remember the three things you needed to survive the camps—luck, help, and smarts. Luck got me into the hospital. Help from Alfred kept me there during the very cold winter of 1944-1945. Whenever a German officer came to inspect the hospital, Alfred knew how to protect me. Because of my malnourishment, a superficial scratch near my ear was slow in healing, and this proved useful. If the inspector was a tough officer who insisted on sending prisoners back to work, Alfred would leave the scratch exposed and tell the officer I was being released the following day and sent back to work. That way I wouldn't be selected. If the officer was more easy going and mostly concerned with counting the prisoners, not killing them, Alfred would wrap bandages around my head and tell him I had a bad head wound. He would even start unwrapping the bandages to show the officer, but the officer would stop him. "No, no. Don't unwrap the wound. Let it heal." With Alfred's help, I remained in the hospital from around the beginning of November until the middle of February. That saved me. I was rested, well fed, and warm. Again, I was very aware that, considering the circumstances, I was privileged. Outside, the temperature was often twenty-five or thirty degrees below zero

Celcius. It was a terrible winter. Through the window, I could see Greek and Italian prisoners working with picks and shovels in the cold, their fingers and noses literally frozen off. It was so bad that one worker allowed the big shovel on a heavy crane to crush his finger so that he'd be sent to the hospital.

Also at the Wüstergiersdorf hospital camp was Felek Lupka. He had been one class behind me at Rumkowski Gymnasium, but was solving mathematical problems one class ahead of me—university-level problems. A brilliant mathematician. One night in the ghetto, I dreamt that Felek and I were in a meadow together. We were wearing striped pajamas. About a week later, I ran into Felek in the street. I told him, "Don't worry. We're going to make it. I saw us wearing pajamas in a meadow." When I became a potato peeler at Kaltwasser, Felek was there too. We walked to the new hospital together, and we slept together on a top bunk. Although not precisely accurate, the dream had already come true. The area around Kaltwasser was like a meadow. We had to walk through fields to get there. The pajamas we wore in the dream were like nothing I had even seen until I saw the striped uniforms worn by Auschwitz prisoners. I had dreamed of camp uniforms. This was my second dream that predicted the future. Unfortunately, my interpretation of the dream was wrong. One day, Alfred said, "Listen, I can't protect both of you guys here forever. There are sick guys in a work *kommando* who need to come here. I'll keep you, Chari, but Felek, you have to go."

"Yes, that's right," Felek said. "I'll go." That was generous of Felek not to make a fuss. When you were discharged from the hospital, you went to the main camp and then…who knows? I never saw Felek again. I don't know if he realized it at the time, but he was politely agreeing to his death sentence.

About a week later, Alfred chose me to be something like an orderly for the room where I slept. I distributed the soup and kept the place clean. Then the sick prisoners from the work detail arrived. Some of them had been Sonders in the ghetto. They had been friends of mine, and now I hardly recognized them. They had a look in their eyes like wild animals. By then, I'd been in the hospital long enough that my nerves had calmed down, but, also, I hadn't been totally traumatized at Kaltwasser. The work on the mountain was hard, but Kaltwasser hadn't been like most camps, where the guards and middle-management prisoners screamed at prisoners and hit them for no reason except to keep them terrified. Looking at my wild-eyed, terrorized friends, I knew it was important that I remain in the hospital as long as possible. Had I been in their work camp, I realized, I would have looked like they did—scared out of the world. The new arrivals were given our room as part of an experiment. They were placed two to a bed, with one guy wearing what was supposedly lice-resistant clothing. It had been treated with something. The Germans wanted to see if the special clothing would protect the prisoner from his bunkmate's lice. I doubt it worked.

My roommates and I moved to a different room. I was still the orderly, responsible for cleanliness, and I kept the new room in shipshape condition. One day, Mengele came for an inspection. There's no doubt it was him. He was tall and polite and well-dressed—immaculately dressed—in an SS officer's uniform. After the war, in the 1960s, I was friends with a Jewish woman who had worked for Mengele in Auschwitz. She painted portraits of prisoners for him. She told me that he was always immaculately dressed and polite. I didn't know much about Mengele, but I knew he was bad. Everyone was scared of him. One time, while inspecting the Kaltwasser work site, he jumped into a ditch and beat a prisoner who wasn't working fast enough. He hit the prisoner with a stick and broke the guy's arm. I didn't see this happen, but the guy with the broken arm soon joined me in the hospital. When Mengele, with two SS men, walked into our room at the hospital, he was wearing white gloves. He ran his fingers along the molding above the door, above eye level, and he found some dust. Of course he found some dust. Like we said in Poland, *jak chcesz psa uderzyć to kija znajdziesz*—if you want to hit the dog, you can always find a stick. Mengele hollered for the block leader, ordered him, "Over the chair," and had an SS man give him five with a stick or belt. The block leader, a Hungarian Jew, was smart. He didn't try to tell Mengele it wasn't his fault. He didn't tell him someone else was in charge of that particular room. However, after Mengele left, the block leader said to me, "I'll give the five back to you." That evening, he gave me the five, the first five I got in the camps. It wasn't that bad. It wasn't with the pants down. I could take it.

The room had twenty beds and only sixteen prisoners. Talk about luxury! Every now and then for dinner, instead of soup, we had boiled potatoes with the skins on. In Poland, we called them *kartofle w mundurkach*—potatoes in uniform.[75] One time, about two weeks after Mengele's visit, Alfred brought potatoes to the room. He handed them to me, a few at a time, and I distributed them to my roommates. There were some extra

---

[75] Today a Polish speaker would probably call them *ziemniaki w mundurkach*.

potatoes, and Alfred instructed me to put them on the four empty beds and, later, to use those potatoes to buy cigarettes for him. There were always some prisoners who could somehow lay their hand on cigarettes, but I didn't get a chance to make the trade. One of my roommates snitched. The Hungarian block leader came in with Alfred and the snitch. The block leader pointed at me and said in German, "You were stealing potatoes for Alfred." The block leader was smart, but so was I. In Auschwitz, I had learned the first commandment of the camps: don't snitch, even if you're in trouble. Snitching won't get you out of trouble—it will only get someone else into trouble.

"No," I said, "I was stealing them for myself."

"You were stealing them for Alfred," he screamed. "Alfred told me so."

Alfred was standing behind the block leader, and I saw him shake his head no.

"I don't know what Alfred said," I answered, "but I was stealing them for myself."

The block leader gave me five strokes again, and he demoted me. He outranked Alfred in the camp hierarchy, and he took away my orderly position. The snitch went out on the next transport. Alfred made sure of that. Being a snitch in camp was like eating poisonous mushrooms. You can do it, but only once.

Two days later, I became an orderly in the doctors' room. This was a promotion. Instead of a room with twenty beds, I was working in a room with six beds for five men. Besides Alfred, there was a Dutch nurse, a French doctor, a Belgian pharmacist, and a doctor whose nationality I can't recall. They knew I could be trusted not to snitch, so they probably asked the chief doctor, a Dutchman, to appoint me. However, the chief doctor and the Hungarian block leader shared a separate room, and it's possible the block leader arranged the promotion because he respected my refusal to snitch. I remember one time going into the operating room, perhaps to take a patient back to his room, and the patient, who was still under light anesthesia, said, "Dr. Boris, ask Chari to give me the potato peels." Dr. Boris, the French physician, turned to me. "Chari, give him some." He knew I would.

I still slept in the room with twenty beds, though. I went into the doctors' room during the day to make their beds, wash their utensils, keep the fire going, and so on. When sick prisoners arrived at the hospital, they were disinfected and given different clothes. As the doctors' orderly, I was able to go into the warehouse and pick through the confiscated clothing. After wearing those flimsy shoes from the ghetto for four months, I finally got some different ones. They were leather and well-oiled, with a square shape and high at the ankles—designed for cross-country skiing. I wore them until the end of the war.

I couldn't have seen it coming, but in February, 1945, my stay at the hospital came to an end. My fortunes were shifting once again. I had lived better than most in the ghetto, but my privileged status as a Sonder disappeared at Auschwitz. I was just another miserable prisoner until I became a potato peeler at Kaltwasser and then, through sheer luck, was transferred to the hospital camp for the winter. That brought three more months of privilege—time to recover from the emotional stress of Auschwitz and the physical stress of Kaltwasser. Time to regain just enough strength, as it turned out, to survive the final two months of the war. Most survivors who walked out of the camps at the war's end had benefited from a camp hospital at some point. Either they had worked in one or spent some time as a patient. If you didn't have some break from the exhausting work in the camps, you weren't likely to make it.

That reminds me of a story that Maniek R., the ghetto electrician, told me after the war. He had been in the Auschwitz hospital with diarrhea when Mengele came in to make a selection. The Jewish physician accompanying Mengele yelled at Maniek, "I told you to get out of here! You're not really sick. You're pretending." He kicked Maniek out. Two days later, all the patients in the hospital were taken to the gas chamber. Maniek had been spared, but he still had diarrhea, so he returned to the hospital. When he saw the physician, Maniek asked, "Why did you do that for me?" The physician told him, "I thought maybe I recognized you from the ghetto." Like I said, besides luck and smarts, you needed help.

I got kicked out of the hospital camp when the Germans liquidated it in early February. With the Russians closing in—they had liberated Auschwitz a month earlier—the Germans evacuated the main camp and satellites of Gross-Rosen.[76] There weren't enough prisoners in our hospital to fill a transport, so we marched west with prisoners from other sub-camps. We totaled about four thousand, and we walked for two days. The SS guards followed us in two military trucks and took turns walking alongside us.

---

[76] In January, 1945, as the Soviets approached, the Germans began to evacuate sub-camps on the eastern bank of the Oder River. The Gross-Rosen main camp was evacuated in early February, followed by the western sub-camps. The Soviets reached the main camp on February 13.

Often, when the Germans evacuated a camp, it turned into a death march. The prisoners—sometimes every single one—died from exhaustion, hunger, and exposure, or the Germans shot them. Our transport was different. The German commandant was a high-ranking noncommissioned SS officer, like a warrant officer or a master sergeant—probably a veteran soldier from the Waffen SS—and he was the kindest guy you could hope to meet under those circumstances. Under any circumstances. We had little or no food, but there were no beatings on the march, no shootings. The commandant wouldn't allow it. No forced running, either. Just easy walking. Some prisoners died from the cold, but there wasn't much he could do about that. The prisoners from the work camps were in pretty bad shape, and the brutal winter wasn't over. On the second evening, we stopped somewhere near the German-Czech border. We sat there in barns for two or three days until a train came for us—compliments of Eichmann.[77] While we waited, the commandant convinced the local farmers to make soup for us. They used tiny potatoes—the kind too small to peel—and didn't put any salt in the soup. Salt was a rare and rationed commodity. At night, I dreamed of having a little heap of salt, a thimble full. That dream didn't come true.

We didn't get salt, but we got bread. Somehow, the commandant arranged bread for us, and we each received two loaves when we boarded the train in the evening. We were told that one loaf was for the three days we would spend on the train. The other loaf, the SS men said, we were "owed" for the previous three days when there had been no bread. That was unheard of. A typical SS officer would have figured, "They survived without bread for three days, so they didn't need it." Of course, we were so hungry that by the next morning we had eaten both loaves. When I tell other survivors that this commandant gave us a back payment of bread and an advance payment for the trip, they don't believe me. I never learned the commandant's name, but I hope the Allies didn't punish him for being in the SS. Anyone who says there were no decent Germans is just plain wrong. Had I met the commandant after the war, I would have thanked him for saving so many lives. Maybe he saved mine.

He also took care of us on the train. No beatings. No shootings. Plenty of water. On some transports, people went crazy from lack of water. When our train stopped, if somebody hollered "water," the commandant would order his SS men to bring around a bucket of water until we were

---

[77] Adolf Eichmann oversaw the trains that carried Jews to the camps.

satisfied. Unheard of! You could even step off the train to relieve yourself. I tried to have a bowel movement, and it was dry and hard. The SS didn't worry too much about prisoners trying to escape. This was Germany and we were Jews—how far could we get? Besides, we were exhausted and it was terribly cold. Prisoners were freezing to death on the train. The sides of the freight cars were only three feet high, and the cars weren't covered. The commandant's kindness wasn't enough. About five hundred of the four thousand didn't make it to our destination—Bergen-Belsen.

Our train transport started in Germany and crossed into Czechoslovakia. Actually, if you had the strength to run, you might have been able to escape in Czechoslovakia. The Czechs were more sympathetic than the Germans, less likely to turn you in. Whenever the train stopped for any length of time in Czechoslovakia, the locals tossed bread and potatoes to us. We crossed back into Germany near the area called Saxon Switzerland, stopped at the Dresden train station and, again, at a big rail yard in Halle, and reached Bergen-Belsen after four nights and three days on the train. When we stopped in Dresden, the city was cordoned off. It was in ruins and still burning.[78] Very recently, just a few years ago, I returned to this area. I traveled by train from Dresden down to Saxon Switzerland and returned by boat on the Elbe River. From the boat, the scenery looked unexpectedly familiar, and then I realized I had been there once before. I started to relive the transport. I forgot I was on a tourist boat. I was back on the open freight cars in the icy wind. I was really affected by this memory, really shook up. It wasn't anger or resentment or fear that I felt. The fear went away some years ago, and I've never had much anger. What I felt on the boat was closer to sadness. It was overwhelming. But there was something else. Back on that cold, miserable transport, it had never occurred to me that one day I would return by first-class train with a German lady on my arm. I guess that's my revenge.

---

[78] The Allies bombed Dresden on February 13 and 14. The bombing pattern was designed to create an enormous firestorm that would maximize human casualties. The fires burned for days. Jörg Friedrich, *The Fire: The Bombing of Germany, 1940-1945* (New York: Columbia University Press, 2006), 310-315.

5

DEATH CAMP

In a death camp, there is nothing but death. Most concentration camps
were labor camps, as the Germans exploited the slave labor of Jews, political
prisoners, criminal prisoners, and prisoners of war. Auschwitz-Berkenau was
both an extermination camp and a labor camp. Some prisoners were gassed
immediately, and others were kept as workers. Bergen-Belsen was a death
camp. It was not an extermination camp in the sense of having gas chambers.
The Germans were not systematically gassing or shooting people. But they
didn't feed you either. They didn't address the problem of typhoid fever.
They just left you to die. Bergen-Belsen was actually a series of camps, and it
was enormous. I was in the "death camp" section of the "men's camp"—
that's how it was called—but the entire place was a death camp.[79]
Krepierungslager. A slow, painful death camp. A death dump. There was no
pretense of usefulness. You went there to die. When International Red
Cross personnel and British troops arrived at Bergen-Belsen, they liberated
sixty thousand prisoners. Twenty-five percent of the sixty thousand died
within two months.[80] One hundred percent would have died if the liberators
had arrived three weeks later. At Bergen-Belsen, there was no hope.

---

[79] In early 1944, Germans began using the Bergen-Belsen "detention camp" as a place to
dump prisoners no longer capable of working. Later that year, the camp began receiving
Jewish prisoners evacuated from camps farther east. Eberhard Kolb, *Bergen-Belsen: From
"Detention Camp" to Concentration Camp, 1943-1945*, translated by Gregory Claeys and
Christine Lattek (Göttingen, Germany: Vandenhoeck and Ruprecht, 1986), 32-34.
[80] On April 15, 1945, the liberated camp held approximately 60,000 prisoners. By June 20,
14,000 of them had died. Kolb, *Bergen-Belsen*, 39-41.

We arrived in the dark. Bergen-Belsen transports usually arrived and departed at night to make things less obvious to the local citizenry. From the train station, we walked for about two miles to the camp. We were already exhausted from the long trip, and the ground was slippery with snow. Five or six prisoners fell and couldn't get up. They were as good as dead. The SS guards left them in the snow to be accounted for the next day. As we approached the camp, I saw clean and neat buildings, with glass windows, and I thought, "Gee, nice buildings, nice camp." Those were the SS buildings, outside the fence. We walked through the gate and it wasn't so nice any more. There were no lights on, indoors or out, but I could tell this was a dirty camp.

The SS guards stayed back and the camp functionaries—lower middle-management German and Polish prisoners—took over. Wielding whips and large clubs, they screamed at us and herded us into five barracks. It was dark and chaotic. It was terrifying. I was tired and just wanted to rest. Inside the barracks, the sleeping facilities were two long, slightly-slanted shelves that came together like a peaked roof. At the peak, wooden boards served as "pillows." There were no blankets. In the darkness, you had to push and shove and find a place on the wooden shelf. When I lay down, I heard a familiar voice on the other side of the peak.

"Beryl?" I asked. Beryl was Berek K., the Sonder who organized even more than I did in the ghetto.

"Oh," he replied, "Tolek." He had gone from the ghetto to Auschwitz to a Gross-Rosen sub-camp, then joined our transport to Bergen-Belsen. The next morning, when I could see Beryl's face, I didn't recognize him. He was so emaciated. He was *Musselman*. He wouldn't last much longer. Clearly, he hadn't spent the winter in a hospital camp.

When I was in the hospital camp, I had met a guy named Heniek K., who was two years older than me. His father had been a Sonder with me, but wasn't chosen for work when we arrived at Auschwitz and, instead, was gassed. Heniek and I became friends and, when we left the hospital, we stuck together. The first night on the train, we took turns sleeping. The one who was awake guarded what was left of our bread. You had to have friends. Actually, there were four of us looking out for each other, keeping each other company, but I can't remember the names of the other two guys. Lying on the shelf in Bergen-Belsen, I invited Beryl to join our little group. He was a witty guy—good company. But he said, "No, I'm here with my people." He never made it out of Bergen-Belsen.

In the morning, they herded us out of the barracks. Immediately, you saw it—*smród, brud i biedota*. Stench, dirt, and poverty. Everywhere you looked, there were corpses. Corpses on carts. Corpses in the mud. I saw camp functionaries pulling gold teeth from the mouths of prisoners who lay helpless and dying. There was a "hospital" barrack where they dumped prisoners who couldn't walk. It wasn't a medical facility, just another place to die. What I saw was a totally hopeless picture. It's impossible to imagine and impossible to describe. Today, I can't really comprehend it. I do know this: in the first few hours at Bergen-Belsen, you lost all hope. Maybe in the first few minutes. You realized that you too would soon be a corpse. Auschwitz was looking better and better. I didn't know the Russians had already liberated it.[81] I wanted to go back there and die cleanly, but nobody was asking me. Without a miracle, I was going to die in the Bergen-Belsen mud.

I got the miracle. Two of them. In the same day. With two miraculous decisions—two lucky guesses—Heniek saved his life and mine.

We were standing in the mud—all 3,500 new arrivals—and the functionaries ordered us to line up in rows of five. Heniek spotted the doctors I had worked for in the hospital camp. They wore red crosses on their sleeves designating them as medical personnel. Heniek said, "Tolek, the doctors always get treated better, and you have a connection with them, so let's stick with them." So our little group of four lined up near the doctors. The functionaries were counting us, dividing us into five groups of seven hundred. These aren't exact numbers, of course, just approximations. The important things is that when they counted us, our row was the last one included in the group with the doctors. That was the first miracle. How close was it? Three of us went with the doctors, but our fourth friend was counted out. They sent him to another group of seven hundred. That would cost him his life.

Now that we were properly counted into five groups, we went back into the five barracks, where we did nothing but wait for the midday soup. I asked the block leader, a Polish Catholic, where we were. When he said Bergen-Belsen, it meant nothing to me. Just an unfamiliar name. I didn't know where in Germany we were, I didn't know the rules of this camp, but I knew the situation was hopeless. Back in the hospital camp, I had organized some sharp-edged pieces of tin shaped halfway between a spoon and a knife. They were useful for cutting bread or a rutabaga. Now I was worried that I could

---

[81] The Soviets reached Auschwitz on January 27, 1945.

get into serious trouble if the tin was mistaken for a knife. I told the block leader what I had, and he told me to drop it on the ground and forget about it. A trivial detail—it's funny the things I remember.

The midday meal was rutabaga soup, the specialty of the camp. We were standing in rows of five in the barrack, and, after everyone had received a soup, the functionaries announced there were a few extra soups. Prisoners in the back started pushing forward, giving the functionaries the excuse they wanted to start hitting us. Somehow, Heniek squeezed to the front and got an extra soup, which he shared with me. He really took care of me that day.

After the soup, we were told that our block, our group of seven hundred, was going to register for work. Why our group and not one of the others, I don't know, but Heniek had gotten us into the right group. We didn't know it was the right group. We didn't know if being sent to work was better or worse than sitting in the barracks. We just did as we were told. We went outside. Some functionaries were sitting at tables, and we had to line up and register with them.[82] I was still exhausted from our transport. I suggested to Heniek that, rather than stand in the long line, we should lie down in the mud and rest, then register after everybody else. Fortunately, Heniek disagreed. "No," he said, "I think we should sign up first and rest later." That was the second miracle. Fortunately, I listened to him. We stood in line, reached the tables, and gave our names and prisoner numbers. They registered the first 500 guys, and Heniek and I made it. We were number 250 or so in the line. The last 200 guys in the line were out of luck. Literally. Totally. They didn't register. They weren't needed. They were sent back inside. The lucky 500 went to the shower.

We didn't know it then, but our death sentences had just been commuted. We had left Gross-Rosen in a group of approximately four thousand, and five hundred had been too weak to survive the trip. At Bergen-Belsen, three thousand were not chosen for work. They remained in camp and died there. Not one survived. Nobody. You can't pretend that, well, if I had been there, I would have found a way to live. You had no chance. That's a death camp.[83] The lucky five hundred who were selected for work spent only twenty-four hours at Bergen-Belsen—at least on this visit—and that saved almost all of us. I'm pretty sure Heniek's idea to stay

---

[82] Rudolf Küstermeier, a German political prisoner, described similar work selections at Bergen-Belsen. Derrick Sington, *Belsen Uncovered* (London: Duckworth, 1946), 113-115.

[83] From early January to April 15, 1945, approximately 35,000 died at Bergen-Belsen, most from starvation and disease due to "systematic neglect." Kolb, *Bergen-Belsen*, 39-42.

with the doctors was complete luck, not smarts. Nobody was making sure the doctors were in the work group. They had to line up and register like the rest of us and just as easily could have been in the back of the line. They got lucky too. Then there was Izio. He and his brother had been firemen in the ghetto, so I knew them. When we went outside to register, a few guys were told to stay in the barrack. They were so obviously weak, so emaciated, that they weren't wanted for work. Izio was one of them. His brother was sent outside to register, and he managed to pull Izio out of the barrack through a window. They both registered and joined the lucky five hundred.

Actually, for the moment, we were 504. I'll get to that. The sunlight was already disappearing when we went to the shower room. It was a large room. Maybe fifty guys showered at a time. There was warm water for about ten minutes. Then they turned on the cold water to chase that bunch out, and the next fifty went in. I'd felt cold water before. No big deal. I even voluntarily took a cold shower in the middle of the night at Kaltwasser. To this day, though, whenever I turn on cold water in the shower, I think of Bergen-Belsen. That's almost daily. Some moments have never left me.

From the shower room, we came out into a dressing area. We found our same clothes, same shoes, freshly disinfected. Once everyone had dressed, SS guards came in and counted us. They counted 504. Four guys had snuck into the work group. That was smarts. In order to catch the four sneaks, the guards called our numbers, one by one. When your number was called, you walked past two SS men, gave your name, and walked through a big doorway back into the shower room. After they had called all 500 numbers, the whole group was in the shower. The four interlopers had disappeared. Or had made it past the guards—don't ask me how. All I know is that the guards were convinced that there were 504 prisoners in the shower. So they repeated the process in the opposite direction—with the same result. There were 504 prisoners in the dressing room, and the guards couldn't identify the four who didn't belong.

They herded us outside into the cold night. I can still see *Lagerkommandant* Kramer standing on a mound, keeping his shiny riding boots out of the mud.[84] He may have been holding a pistol. He announced, "If I catch the four guys, I'll shoot them like dogs. But you step forward now, and I'll let you go back to the barracks, no questions asked." No one stepped

---

[84] Josef Kramer took over command of the camp in December, 1944. Kolb, *Bergen-Belsen*, 37.

forward. No one that stupid would have made it this far. So the guards just picked four guys—four very unlucky guys—and sent them to the barracks.

I don't remember getting an evening soup that day, but I guess I shouldn't complain. I was walking out of a death camp. We marched back to the train station, sat on the train for some hours, then departed in the early morning before the sun came up. The trip was only two hours and we were in closed boxcars. No one was freezing to death. There was one passenger car for the SS men, including the commandant—the same guy who looked out for us on the trip from Gross-Rosen. He was going to be in charge at our work camp! Maybe that was a miracle too.

Next stop: Hildesheim, a medium-sized German town. We arrived in the morning and walked for ten minutes to the center of town. Our destination was a municipal building previously used for town festivities. We entered a large room with all the furniture removed. This was our new camp. We were elated. The day before we had been sitting in the dirty, cramped barracks of a death camp, and now we were being housed in a reception hall. Can you imagine?! Everyone got two blankets and some sort of pillow. There was room to stretch out and there was straw on the floor, or maybe we had straw-filled mattresses. It was really nice, so much better than the other camps, but I don't remember all the details. My memory is good but short. Whatever the details, this was not a place for dying. We were there as laborers. Allied bombers had hit the Hildesheim train station, an important freight depot, and the Germans wanted it rebuilt. We provided simple manual labor—filling in bomb craters and clearing debris off the tracks. The railway administration provided our living conditions and paid the SS to make us available for work. The Germans were desperate for labor. They needed to keep the trains running. They weren't going to starve us to death. There wouldn't be selections for transport back to Bergen-Belsen. And, with the good SS man in charge of our camp, there would be no terrorizing.

We had a normal camp life. We started feeling like humans again. In the morning, we got something warm to drink, then walked a short distance to the rail yard where we worked. There was a break for the midday soup, which was thick with vegetables and potatoes. It wasn't watery like at other camps. In the evening, back in the reception hall—no, it wasn't a champagne buffet. We got a warm meal, bread, and a *zulage*. If you were smart, you saved some bread for the morning. If there was a complaint, it was that the reception hall had only four or five toilets for five hundred men returning from work at the same time. Actually, the only ones who complained about conditions at Hildesheim were the SS men. We were accustomed to living on bread and soup, but the SS guards had higher expectations and no one was providing them with good German food. They complained to our kapos that the railway took care of us while SS men had to scavenge for food because the *Wehrmacht* wouldn't feed them. Back in the ghetto, we had deduced that the Germans were losing the war, but I had figured it would take a long time. Now we had clues that the war's end was near. The SS men were uneasy. The train station had been bombed. We were receiving better treatment. Maybe there was reason for hope after all.

Don't misunderstand me—we weren't on vacation. We still were prisoners, performing forced labor, under armed guard. When we weren't working, we were under SS supervision at the reception hall. In the mornings, the *Volkspolizei* came to collect us for work. The *Volkspolizei* were militiamen, either too young or too old to be soldiers—under seventeen or over seventy—or they were wounded *Wehrmacht* veterans. None of these guys were SS. They weren't trained to be cruel. Mostly, they hadn't been trained for anything. They were just given a gun and told to watch us. One time, after we finished filling in a bomb crater, a guard told our *kommando* to relax. It was about thirty minutes before quitting time, too late to start a new task. The guard was about twenty-five years old, probably a veteran of the Russian front. A second guard, maybe age thirty-five, objected. He insisted that it was their patriotic duty to keep us working.

He asked, "Don't you feel any responsibility to the Fatherland?"

The younger guard pulled up a pant leg, revealing a war wound. "Don't tell me about patriotic duty," he said. We didn't work anymore that day.

Some of the *Volkspolizei* could be decent like that, but their boss was mean. In a similar situation, just before quitting time, the boss decided we had to keep laboring. He ordered us to carry stones, two at a time, from one pile to another. Still, compared to most work camps, never mind a death camp, this was a vacation. Without the constant terrorizing, without the screaming and hitting and killing, we stopped being afraid. We didn't have the wild animal look in our eyes. And we weren't going to die of "natural causes"—disease, starvation, exhaustion. At the Hildesheim camp, you could live forever.

You could live because there were opportunities to organize food. And we were good at it. The war was over four years old, and any Jew who had lasted that long—in the ghetto, in the camps—knew how to survive. We were five hundred guys who knew how to take the initiative, knew how to smuggle food into camp. The only ones in our way were third-rate SS guards and poorly-trained *Volkspolizei*. They were no match for us. When we were working, each of us kept a small tin can, about one-quart size, tied to his belt. During lunch break, the midday soup was poured into your can. If you didn't finish your soup, you were allowed to bring the leftovers back to camp to eat in the evening. Why wouldn't a hungry prisoner finish his soup? Because it provided a means for organizing additional food. At the rail yard, we found food in bomb-damaged train cars. We would put the cottage cheese or sugar or whatever it was into the tin can, cover the food with a piece of cardboard, and put thick soup on top, maybe the last inch or so. There was no problem getting that past the guards. If they knew about it, they didn't care. We also hid potatoes and vegetables in our jacket sleeves, which we tied tight at the wrists. When we returned to the reception hall, the SS men would casually pat us down. They weren't real thorough. We held our arms out from our sides, and they missed the food in our sleeves.

I'm not saying this was entirely without danger. Organizing was not officially permitted, and there were different degrees of tolerance. If a food container had been damaged and broken open, the guards usually didn't care if you took the contents. If the container was undamaged, if the food was clearly not contaminated, then it was definitely off-limits to us. In between was a gray area, like if a can was dented but not broken open. You had to know what you could get away with. Still, only one of our five hundred suffered a serious punishment for organizing. The mean *Volkspolizei* boss caught an eighteen-year-old Hungarian Jew with an unopened can of green beans. I saw him lead the young prisoner to a bomb crater and order him to kneel down. Then, *genickschuss*.[85] The *Volkspolizei* boss shot the kid in the back of the head. After the war, I heard the man was sentenced to five years in prison.

People sometimes ask me if, when I was a prisoner, I had a desire for revenge, if I ever thought about making the Germans pay for how they treated us. No, I never thought of committing some atrocity. I never dreamed of physical vengeance. My only thoughts of revenge came at Hildesheim. When we walked between the reception hall and the freight yard, we saw townspeople, dressed normally, going about their lives. One day, the thought occurred to me that if I was liberated right then, I would walk into the closest house, tell the family to heat a tub of water, and I would

---

[85] Execution-style murder with a bullet to the back of the neck.

wash myself and get some decent clothes without lice. That was my idea of revenge. I never felt hatred toward the Germans. I still don't. When we had the lessons on hating, I must have been absent. See, if you hate, you don't just hate one group. If you hate Jews, you probably also hate blacks, Gypsies, whomever. The problem is you, not them. You're the one with the hate.

One thing I did learn from my experiences in the ghetto and the camps was if you tell a lie, you cannot hesitate. You must lie without thinking. At Hildesheim, I decided that if I was ever caught doing something not permitted and was asked for my prisoner number, I would give a false number. The guards were so lax, I figured I could get away with it. At Kaltwasser, we had been assigned prisoner numbers, but they weren't tattooed into our skin or even sewn onto our jackets. We were just ordered to remember them and, of course, the Germans wrote them down. I received 17596. That was the number I used at Bergen-Belsen when I registered for work. But I had another number in my head. Before the war, my family's telephone number was 17814. That sounded like a prisoner number and I knew it well. I could say it without thinking. I had my lie ready.

One day, the *Volkspolizei* guards caught ten or fifteen of us in a damaged train car, digging into barrels of cottage cheese. The barrels were already open when we found them, but the guards couldn't be sure of that. They demanded our numbers. I didn't hesitate. 17814. That evening, after roll call in the reception hall, the SS guards called out the numbers the *Volkspolizei* had taken down. The guilty prisoners stepped forward for punishment. It wasn't bad—five or ten swats on the ass with a light stick. It wasn't a baseball bat. You didn't have to drop your pants. The *Volkspolizei* had reported the incident, so the SS had to administer some sort of punishment, but probably the kind commandant told them to go easy. Still, when they called out 17814, I didn't move. After all, that wasn't my prisoner number. The guards threatened double or triple punishment for number 17814 if he didn't step forward immediately. They insisted they would find him. I suppose if they had been serious, they could have beaten the other guilty guys until someone identified the missing culprit, but they didn't pursue it. Or maybe, to this day, they're still looking for me over there. People ask me, what if there had been a prisoner at Hildesheim with number 17814? Wouldn't I have put him into serious trouble? First of all, back then, it never crossed my mind. And second, even if it had, my ass was sweeter than his. You protected your ass first. That was the attitude in the camps.

I avoided a minor punishment that time because of smarts. The next time was a different story. The title of the story is The Scariest Moment of My Life. Naturally, it had to do with food. One afternoon at work, I was clearing broken wood from train tracks atop a ridge. I worked my way to the edge of the ridge and looked down into the backyard of an abandoned house. The house had been damaged by the impact of bombs on the nearby train station. The windows and doors were blown out—that sort of thing. It wasn't totally destroyed. I suspect the occupants had cleared out the cupboards and taken their food stores with them. The food they considered unfit for human consumption they had left behind in their yard. I hurried down the slope and picked through spoiled preserves and half-rotten potatoes and onions. I opened two or three jars of preserves, scraped aside the layer of mold, and ate the good jam beneath it. There was lots of food in the yard, but I didn't have time to eat more. I filled my soup can to the top with jam. I hid potatoes and onions in my pants legs and tied the legs at the ankles. Then I climbed back up the slope. The *Volkspolizei* guard who watched our twenty-man *kommando* hadn't noticed my absence. As there was little chance of a poorly-fed, poorly-dressed, foreign Jew escaping in Germany, the guard just stood with his rifle and didn't pay much attention.

I resumed gathering wood, careful not to spill the jam. Eventually, the guard noticed something suspicious. I was picking up wood with only one hand, tucking the pieces under the opposite arm, because the other hand was holding the tin can upright. The guard called to me, "What do you have there?" I showed him the tin can—I really had no choice. He took his rifle off his shoulder, moved the bolt into firing position, and aimed it at me. I was staring into a loaded rifle from five yards away. An awful feeling came over me. I'd suffered through so much, the end of the war seemed near, and now I'm going to be shot. I remember it like it happened thirty minutes ago, not over sixty years ago. He said, *"Ich knall dich über den Haufen"*—"I'll shoot you like a dog."[86] My life flashed before my eyes—that really happens—and I started talking. Fast. I don't remember it as a voluntary response.

"I found it outside," I told him, "behind a house. I didn't enter the house." I knew that a few days earlier the Hildesheim police or Gestapo had hanged four conscripted Slav workers for entering a house in Hildesheim to

---

[86] The literal translation is "I'll shoot you over a trash heap."

organize food.[87] The Germans had zero tolerance for that. I kept talking. "The jam was thrown away. It was moldy. The people left it behind." Fortunately, there was a little mold on the jam in the can. I showed him. "See. Look. It's moldy." I was speaking very proper, respectful German, and he was listening. Thank goodness for that tough German teacher before the war! Meanwhile, potatoes and onions had begun falling from my pants.

Next comes the important part. The guard didn't shoot me. He didn't beat me. He didn't even order me to drop the food. He shouldered the rifle and said, "Be careful. Don't let them catch you with that when you return to camp." That was it. I was free to go. I shared the food with Heniek and my doctor friends from the hospital camp. They said I looked frightened and pale, probably the same way I looked at Kaltwasser when I almost got caught with a jacket filled with potatoes. I'm still amazed. I was face to face with death, and the German guard—it was his duty to punish me, even though the food had been discarded—but instead of pulling the trigger, he expressed genuine concern. Unbelievable? Only if you think there weren't any good Germans. Without good Germans, though, I wouldn't be here to tell this story. He was a decent guy stuck in an indecent job. He didn't want to shoot me, and my fast talking, my explanation, gave him a way out. My passable German allowed me to communicate with him, and that probably made me more human in his eyes. That's how I understand it, anyway. Other survivors criticize me for being pro-German, but I'm only describing what I saw. This is my experience.

Not all Germans were bad, and not all Jewish prisoners were good. The kapo of my *kommando* at Hildesheim was a big, well-fed Hungarian Jew named Fischer. He was easily over six feet tall. I first noticed him when he came out of the shower in Bergen-Belsen. Some prisoners were sitting on a table in the dressing area, and he pushed one off. "I'm sitting there now," he announced. That's how Kapo Fischer was—big, intimidating, and mean. Once during the midday break at Hildesheim, a German railway employee had an extra barrel of soup for our commando, but Kapo Fischer wouldn't let us have it. "They didn't work hard enough today," he told the German. "They don't deserve an extra soup."

---

[87] The four men were hanged in the old market square. A sign on the gallows announced, "They plundered." Andrew Bergerson, *Ordinary Germans in Extraordinary Times: The Nazi Revolution in Hildesheim* (Bloomington: Indiana University Press, 2004), 229.

Later, one of the *Volkspolizei* guards remarked, "Gosh, he's your own kind. How can he be so mean to you?"

When we found a barrel of condensed milk, Kapo Fischer gave everyone in the *kommando* a mere spoonful—just a lick—and kept the rest for himself. I remember thinking, "If I survive the war, instead of a water cooler, I'll have a cooler of condensed milk." Maybe it was a silly fantasy, but it shows how at Hildesheim, despite the cruelty of Kapo Fischer and the *Volkepolizei* boss, I had regained some hope for the future.

Also working at the Hildesheim train station were British, French, and Polish prisoners of war. You could tell they were POWs from how they were dressed, how the guards treated them, and how they responded to the guards. They weren't as degraded as Jewish prisoners. The Gurkhas were the most impressive.[88] They were spic-and-span. They came to work with shoes polished and uniforms buttoned. They folded their jackets and placed them neatly in two rows while they were working. They maintained military discipline. I once saw a German guard trying to get them to finish filling a bomb crater, and they ignored him. "Come on," he said, "it will only take a few minutes, and then we won't have to come back here." But it was noon, the Gurkhas had quit for lunch, and, anyway, they wouldn't take orders from him. They only operated through their chain of command, so the German would have to discuss it with their officer. The Gurkhas were prisoners only in flesh, not in spirit. They were soldiers doing a job and seemed totally oblivious to the situation around them. The French and Polish POWs didn't have that kind of discipline or focus, although the French guys sometimes tossed food to us.

The other guys who really impressed me were the Greek Jews. In the camps, there were different degrees of national loyalty. At Auschwitz, most camp functionaries were Poles, and they treated Polish Jews a little better—or a little less worse—than they treated French or Hungarian Jews. A Hungarian Jew had been the head prisoner at the Wüstergiersdorf hospital camp, and Kapo Fischer was the dominant prisoner at Hildesheim. They both looked out for their fellow Hungarians and were less sympathetic to Polish Jews. According to Primo Levi, though, the Greek prisoners had the strongest solidarity, and I agree.[89] There were a few Greek Jews in our group of five

---

[88] Gurkhas, from Nepal, served in the British Army.

[89] Primo Levi, *Survival in Auschwitz: The Nazi Assault on Humanity* (New York: Collier, 1961), 64-65 and 72.

hundred at Hildesheim, and they really stuck together. They were also the most resourceful prisoners. One time we were standing in line for the midday soup, and the Greeks were walking along the line handing out candy! Where did they get candy? Why didn't they feel a need to stand in line for soup? I don't know. They were Greeks. Some of us concluded that the four guys who snuck into our group in the Bergen-Belsen shower must have been Greeks. Of course they were Greeks. Who else had the audacity to try and the cleverness to avoid getting caught?

We were taken to Hildesheim to clean up after Allied bombings, but the Allies weren't finished. There was another air raid shortly after we arrived. It was minor. We were working at the train station when the alarm sounded. We went to an open field, away from any buildings that might be targeted. The *Volkspolizei* were scared stiff. They lied down in the field and covered their heads and butts with helmets. At the far end of the field was a Gestapo office, and the Gestapo men were also lying in the field. As for the prisoners, we weren't bothered at all. There was nothing to be scared of. The bombers weren't trying to kill *us*.[90] We sat upright and picked at lice or sewed on buttons or whatever. For us, it was a nice break from work. When the raided ended, there was total disorder, yet none of our group ran away. We looked for our guards. We were lost without them. This was Germany—who else would take care of us, where else would we go? After the guards concluded that all prisoners were accounted for, another twenty guys showed up. That's how disorganized things were.

One final bombing came a few days after the scary moment with the preserves. Once again, the alarm sounded and we went to the open field and took a break. But this was a big bombing. The entire town was left in rubble and hundreds were dead.[91] For days afterward, you could smell the decomposing bodies. At the freight yard, boxcars had been thrown atop buildings and the bomb craters were two stories deep. Nine or ten prisoners hadn't gone to work at the train station that day. They were too sick to work,

---

[90] In a bombing zone, prisoners can be "strangely at peace" because they don't interpret the attack as a personal affront, and because they feel no obligation to fight back. For guards, the situation is reversed and, thus, more likely to be traumatic. Dave Grossman, *On Killing: The Psychological Cost of Learning to Kill in War and Society* (Boston: Back Bay Books, 1995), 57-58.

[91] In 1945, the Allies bombed the Hildesheim freight yard on February 22, March 3, and March 14-15. On March 22, a much larger attack—235 planes, 446 tons of bombs, in 18 minutes—destroyed the city and killed over 1,700 in a city of 72,000. Friedrich, *The Fire*, 184-186.

or maybe they were cleaning our camp. Either way, they all died when a bomb leveled our reception hall accommodations. When I returned to Hildesheim in the late 1970s, I tried to find the location of our old sleeping quarters. I asked at city hall and was told, "We never had a concentration camp here."

"Yes, I understand," I replied, "but I was in it." They sent me to the assessor's office, where I received directions to the site. The reception hall had been rebuilt as a retirement home.

With the reception hall destroyed, we relocated to a meadow near the river and slept in the open air. Fortunately, the March weather was mild and dry. The next morning, we went right back to work cleaning up the freight yard. Only recently did it occur to me that I could have hid in the bombed-out train station and survived on food from the station cafeteria. Of course, the food wouldn't have been refrigerated. Eventually, I would have become ill or hungry and then…who knows? Anyway, a day or two after the air raid, I decided to bathe in the river after work. The sun had been shining all day, so I thought the river would be warm. Stupid me. When the coast was clear, I took off my clothes, stepped into the water, and turned blue. It was like ice. I couldn't jump right back out because some couples—German civilians— were walking along the bank. I was afraid to be seen naked—the SS would punish me for offending the master race. It was five or ten minutes before I could emerge unseen and get dressed while dripping wet.

That was the end of our stay in comfortable Hildesheim. We were no longer needed there. The train station was beyond easy repair and our camp was in ruins. Four or five days after the bombing, the kind SS commandant took us out of town. That was a bad deal. The bombing hadn't done us any favors. After a few weeks of the easy life, we were heading for a serious work camp in Ahlem, a suburb of Hanover. It was a half-day's walk to the north.[92] The camp looked nice, with five neat barracks and a roll call area. It was nothing like dirty Bergen-Belsen or bombed-out Hildesheim. It was a clean camp. But it was tough. Very tough.

When we approached in the late afternoon, we called back and forth to the prisoners behind the wire to sniff each other out. Most of them were wearing striped camp uniforms. We asked who they were, and they said

---

[92] On March 26, 1945, around 500 prisoners from the *Stadthalle* in Hildesheim arrived in Ahlem. Rainer Fröbe, et al, *Konzentrationslager in Hannover: KZ-Arbeit und Rüstungsindustrie in der Spätphase des Zweiten Weltkriegs* (Hildesheim: Verlag August Lax, 1985), Vol. 1, 396.

"Łódźers"—Polish Jews from Łódź. That was good news to us Łódźers and not so good news for the Hungarian Jews in our group. But Ahlem, it turned out, was not like Kaltwasser or Hildesheim, where all the prisoners in camp were Jews. Outside the wires, the guards were real SS, not wounded veterans or elderly *Volkspolizei*. Inside, the camp was run by greeners—German criminal prisoners identified by green triangles. They were the upper management. The middle management were Łódźers in charge of small work details. The Łódźers told us about the greeners. They said the chief prisoner—the *Lagerälteste*—had cut up his mother-in-law, put her in a suitcase, and sent it to his wife as a birthday present. The head of the camp police—the *Lagerkapo*—was a small Austrian sonofabitch who had spent twelve years in prison before the war. These were not nice guys.

Heniek and I were still sticking together. There were two to three hundred guys in each barrack, and we slept two to a bunk. Our block leader was a real quiet greener. He didn't hit or scream. He didn't harass us. You just had to stay out of his way. He had a *pipel*, which means a personal servant or errand boy. The block leader also used the *pipel* to satisfy his sexual needs. The first evening, the *pipel* asked me, "Don't I know you from the ghetto?" Maybe he had seen me there—Sonders were prominent individuals—but I didn't recognize him. He was four or five years younger than me. Still, I pretended like I knew him because I thought he might be a useful connection. Maybe there was a thread left of my father's coattails. Actually, it was Heniek's idea. He said, "If the guy thinks he knows you, see what you can get out of it." The *pipel* told me to come back after the evening soup was distributed and he'd share any leftovers with me. Which he did. In fact, almost every evening, he let me clean out the soup barrel. I scraped the dregs into my bowl and shared them with Heniek. Like I said, in the camps it was important to have friends, and the Łódźers were looking out for each other.

Kapo Fischer, the big Hungarian Jew, was in trouble, and the Łódźers weren't going to help him. On that first night, the *Lagerkapo* asked in one of the other barracks who was the toughest prisoner from Hildesheim. They told him Kapo Fischer. We were already lying in our bunks when the *Lagerkapo*, with two or three helpers, entered our block and called out, "Kapo Fischer!" There was no response. Fischer was sharing a bunk with the Hungarian Jew who had been the head prisoner at the hospital camp. Their privileged days were over. "I'll find you, Fischer," the *Lagerkapo* said. "You'd better come out." Fischer crawled out of his bunk and the *Lagerkapo* led him away. "You come with me," we heard the little Austrian say. "If you're lucky, you'll come back. But very few are lucky."

The greeners wanted us to know from Day One who was boss. They didn't want to be challenged. So they killed Kapo Fischer. One of the minor camp functionaries—an assistant cleaning boy or something—knew me from the ghetto, and he told me what happened. The greeners took Fischer to the washroom and tried to beat him to death. They knocked him out but couldn't kill him. The big Hungarian was too tough. They summoned the *Lagerälteste*, and he told the *Lagerkommandant*, the noncommissioned SS officer who oversaw the camp, that Kapo Fischer had been inciting Jews to escape. The SS man shot and killed Kapo Fischer, and we got the message: The greeners were in charge. Jews were just there to work.

Our job at Ahlem was digging tunnels for an underground facility for Continental Tires and other companies. That's what we were told. It wasn't nearly as bad as the construction work at Kaltwasser. First, we didn't have to walk up a mountain every morning. The work site was practically across the street from the camp. Second, we worked in tunnels, protected from the elements, and spring was coming on. We didn't have to worry about our hands freezing to steel rails. Third, we had the night shift and weren't closely supervised. The Germans thought that non-Jewish prisoners—Poles, Ukrainers, Russians—were more likely to escape, so only Jews worked at night. We slept in the barracks during the day, woke up for an evening soup, then walked to the tunnels. The greeners were back in camp, the SS guards remained at the tunnel entrances, and our only real supervision was from a German civilian foreman, who wasn't real interested in watching Jews move dirt. There were two other foremen. One was a German political prisoner— a red triangle, not a greener. The other was the only Gypsy I ever saw in the camps. Before I had arrived at Auschwitz, the Germans had killed all the Gypsies there to make room for transports of Hungarian Jews. A few Gypsies had already been sent out to smaller work camps. Maybe that's how this guy survived. I don't know. But somehow he became something like a sub-kapo. He knew how to look tough. He talked big. He screamed at prisoners. He threatened us with a big stick, like a baseball bat. Only he never hit anyone. He and the red triangle prisoner weren't real enforcers, so Heniek and I didn't do much work. After the break for midnight soup, we would hide in a dark corner and take a nap. Around two or three a.m., the German foreman would check on the workers. If he caught us and told us to get back to work, we'd find another dark corner. Around five or six a.m., we'd wake up and join the other workers. It was a pretty good schedule.

One time, though, we overslept. That wasn't good. When I woke up, I heard our co-workers calling for us. They were already assembled and counted and ready to return to camp. Heniek and I were in trouble. If we stayed in the tunnel, the Germans would accuse us of attempting to escape. If we said we weren't trying to escape, that we simply fell asleep, that would bring punishment too. Fortunately, an idea came to me. You've got to think on your feet and tell lies without hesitation. As we ran to join the group, I told Heniek we should loosen our pants and let them fall. When we reached the entrance, the Gypsy asked where we'd been. He had his stick ready.

"We have diarrhea," I said. "We were sitting on the barrels." There were barrels in the tunnel for this purpose.

"Why didn't you come?"

"We came as fast as we could." He could see us pulling up our pants, and I guess that convinced him. There was no punishment. No one reported our tardiness to the SS. My quick thinking had worked, but it's a good thing our friends called for us, a good thing we made it to the entrance before they left for camp. If the Germans thought you were attempting to escape, they shot or hung you the same day.

How do I rate Ahlem? How many stars do I give the camp? It was better than Kaltwasser, where they worked you to death, and worse than Hildesheim, where you could survive. If the greeners at Ahlem decided to punish a prisoner—for any infraction—they usually killed him. That's how the camp stayed orderly and clean. That's how the greeners kept their privileges. But if you stayed out of their way and did as they ordered, they left you alone. The biggest problem at Ahlem was that we couldn't organize food. There were no kitchens in the tunnels, and the greeners controlled food distribution in the camps. When the camp first opened, some Jewish prisoners had received low-level functionary positions and maybe they had access to extra food, but newcomers were out of luck.[93] The soup was enough to keep us alive for a while, and the work wasn't too bad. We had arrived rested and nourished from our stay at Hildesheim. But could we have lasted on two soups a day for six months? I don't know.

---

[93] The Ahlem camp was opened in November, 1944. Fröbe, et al, *Konzentrationslager in Hannover*, 353-354.

I should mention the beets. Before the war, I didn't like cooked beets, but somehow I ate them. In the ghetto, I found I couldn't tolerate cooked beets at all. Sometimes our midday soup contained pickled beets, and I just couldn't eat it, no matter how hungry I was. One time, my grandmother gave me rutabaga pancakes, and thirty minutes later I threw up. She confessed they were really beet pancakes. She had burned them to disguise the beet color. In Ahlem, the soup sometimes included beets, and I had to give mine to Heniek. As bad as life was in the work camp, cooked beets were worse.

We were only at Ahlem for about two weeks. With the Allies closing in, the Germans were evacuating the smaller camps. Our camp was liquidated near the start of April, and the underground facility was left unfinished. As we departed, the SS guards fled in a hurry as the British were near.[94] However, they found time to set fire to the camp infirmary, which held those prisoners too weak to walk. Local Germans extinguished the fire and cared for the sick prisoners until British troops arrived. I know this because Sosiek, one of my distant relatives—his brother had married my aunt—was among the sick. I saw him when we first arrived at Ahlem, but I barely recognized him because he was so emaciated. It was easier for him to recognize me. After the war, I found him in a Hanover hospital. He had made it, but his brother had died in the Ahlem camp.

Our transport out of Ahlem was under the supervision of the good commandant, the same SS man who had taken us from Gross-Rosen to Bergen-Belsen, then to Hildesheim, and Ahlem. At least it wouldn't be a death march. We encountered other transports on the road, and those guys weren't so fortunate. They had to walk fast—they usually passed us—and the guards shot whoever couldn't keep up. When you heard a shot, you didn't turn and look. There was no reason. It was nothing unusual. If you heard "Oy!" it was a Polish Jew. If you heard "Yoy!" it was Hungarian Jew or maybe a Romanian. Our commandant didn't allow shooting. He didn't insist on fast walking. He arranged food for us on the road. Approximately six hundred prisoners departed from Ahlem, and only one died on the four-day march. That was the good news. The bad news was that the Germans were transporting all the prisoners from the small camps in the region to one place: Bergen-Belsen. With the end of the war in sight, we were going back to the death camp. We were being sent there to die.

---

[94] The Ahlem camp was liquidated on April 6, 1945. Fröbe, et al, *Konzentrationslager in Hannover*, 399.

Some prisoners escaped. It wasn't too difficult. We weren't locked in train cars. There was no roll call. It was just six hundred prisoners walking through the countryside, sleeping in barns at night. The commandant wouldn't even let his men shoot a fleeing prisoner. His attitude was, "you're bigger than they are—just run after them and bring them back." Most of the greeners got away. They were Germans, adequately nourished, and had organized civilian clothing back in Ahlem. They could easily slip away and pass as civilians. I don't know what became of them, though I heard the Austrian *Lagerkapo* was captured after the war and put back in prison. Jewish prisoners couldn't blend in, and, if they were like me, escape never entered their minds. I mean, where would you go? That was the attitude. We were generally passive. A few did try to escape—there was little to lose. One night, two brothers from Łódź disappeared. Their name was Gelbart. One had been a Sonder and was an acquaintance of mine. I don't remember his first name. His brother, who I didn't know, was a pharmacist at the Sonder headquarters. After they escaped, they became separated. The pharmacist managed to survive in the woods, and British soldiers eventually rescued him. I ran into him at a Displaced Persons camp after the war. The other Gelbart didn't stay in the woods. He came out of hiding, found another transport, and told them he'd gotten lost. He walked with them to Bergen-Belsen.

On the first day of the march, our group walked through Hanover. I remember there weren't many people around. After two days of walking, we somehow ended up behind enemy lines. The British were that close. We stopped in a village and spent the night in four or five barns. The next morning, the commandant was in no hurry to get going. We didn't know what was going on. We didn't find out about being in British-held territory until later. But I think the commandant was hoping that British troops would find us and that the prisoners would attest to his decency. We were so close to being rescued and not returning to the death camp. So close. Unfortunately, we never saw British troops. The *Wehrmacht* sent a lieutenant to find us. He outranked the commandant, took charge of our transport, and led us back to German-held territory. When the *Wehrmacht* officer first showed up, one of my Sonder friends from the ghetto went to him and said, "I can't go any farther." The officer pulled out a pistol and shot him. I didn't see it, but I heard the gunshot, and later someone told me the officer had shot Reichenbach. The poor guy's wife was at Bergen-Belsen, and, after the war, I told her what had happened. She had to know.

I wasn't as desperate as Reichenbach. I was still wearing the high top shoes from the hospital camp, and they were in good shape. We were walking perhaps fifteen miles per day, but the conditions in early April were mild. I remember the commandant allowing us to lie down on the side of the road for thirty minutes—a much-needed break. I think this is when the transport with Ukrainers came by. The guards were German and Ukraine SS men, and Ukrainers were very anti-Semitic. As they passed, I saw a Jewish prisoner pull a piece of bread from his pocket. Immediately, a Ukrainer prisoner grabbed him and shouted, in German, "Hey, he stole my bread." A Ukrainer guard hit the Jewish prisoner—no questions asked—and the Ukrainer prisoner got the bread.

As we sat on the roadside, we chewed grass from the field—wheat or rye or something. It was already about a foot high and tasted so sweet and refreshing. I was reasonably nourished and rested, though, compared to many of the prisoners on the way to Bergen-Belsen. In fact, all the guys who had been at Hildesheim were doing okay. This is an important point. If you worked as hard as the Germans demanded and ate as little as they provided, you would die in the camps. You needed luck, help, and smarts to avoid that fate. Yes, I had it bad, but only for short periods of time, otherwise I wouldn't have made it. Up to that moment, I had only worked hard for four or five weeks, and they weren't consecutive. I had breaks in between. That was critical. I didn't get much to eat at Auschwitz, but I didn't do any work there either. At Kaltwasser, we had a little more food and spent two or three more weeks doing nothing. Then, two weeks or so of hard work on the mountain almost killed me. I was saved by becoming a potato peeler, and I recovered during the winter at the Wüstergiersdorf hospital camp. Next came the miracles that got me out of Bergen-Belsen and into Hildesheim, where the work was easy and the food sufficient. Finally, another two weeks or so of serious work and insufficient food at Ahlem. But even there, Heniek and I had the occasional extra soup and slept on the job. So you can say that for much of my time in the camps I was cheating the Germans. I don't apologize.

And then we got back to Bergen-Belsen.[95] The train station was north of the camp, and this time we were walking in from the south, so the approach looked different. As we walked along the highway, we saw signs

---

[95] Kolb, *Bergen-Belsen*, 39, says that the death marches from labor camps near Hanover began arriving at Bergen-Belsen on April 8, 1945.

warning German civilians: stay away, high security area, military training ground, you'll be shot on sight. This suggested a military installation was nearby, which was true. There was a major military training facility, which conveniently camouflaged the presence of a death camp.[96] We didn't know where we were headed until, on the fourth or fifth evening, we reached the gate. They herded us into the same section as before—the "death camp" part of the death camp. No roll call, no counting. Why bother? Everyone was going to die soon.

The next morning, under orders from the camp functionaries, we started dragging corpses to the mass graves.[97] I've already explained what that was like. Walking corpses pulling lifeless corpses. Corpses everywhere you looked. The camp wasn't muddy like in February, but it was still very dirty and filled with disease. The lice carried typhoid fever, and, within a few days, our clothes were so lice-ridden that if you undressed, your pants would stand up and walk off on their own. If I rubbed my hand over my neck, I would fill my hand with lice. I was so deeply bitten on the chest that for two or three years afterward you could still see the de-pigmented areas. The wounds had turned into lighter skin. But I was lucky. The first louse I encountered during the war gave me typhoid fever. That was back in the ghetto, where I received decent medical attention thanks to my father's coattails. After I recovered, I was immune to typhoid, which was a good thing to be, particularly in Bergen-Belsen. Actually, dying in Bergen-Belsen wouldn't have been so bad. Living there was awful beyond words.

One thing was different from my previous stay at Bergen-Belsen. Then there was no hope. I was saved only by miracles. Now, somehow, there was a glimmer of hope. We knew that Allied troops were in the area. We hoped they would liberate us. We hoped that we would still be alive when they reached the camp. A glimmer of hope, but only a glimmer. Death was everywhere. Even the pretense of a "hospital" barrack was gone. We didn't like our chances.

At first, we received some bread and an evening soup. Then *Lagerkommandant* Kramer stopped dispensing bread. We had to live—die—

---

[96] British planners interpreted their aerial photographs of Bergen-Belsen as showing different sections of the military camp, not a concentration camp. Hagit Lavsky, *New Beginnings: Holocaust Survivors in Bergen-Belsen and the British Zone in Germany, 1945-1950* (Detroit: Wayne University Press, 2002), 42.

[97] According to Kolb, *Bergen-Belsen*, 46, the corpse-dragging began on April 11, as the camp administrators knew they would soon be surrendering the camp to the British.

on thin rutabaga soup. No fat, no protein, no nothing. At some point, the camp water system failed and wasn't fixed.[98] We couldn't get a drink if we needed one. Heniek and I split up during the day, hoping to get different jobs, or at least drag corpses on different routes, to increase our chances of organizing food. About the only possibility was to grab a handful of potato peels from a cart pulled by prisoners. We hid the peels in our clothing and shared them in the evening—after wiping off the lice. One evening, I proudly pulled out some peels. "Heniek, I got these for you." He produced three beets, an astonishing find. They were raw, so I could tolerate them. Our cooperation, plus arriving at Bergen-Belsen in decent shape, is how we survived while so many were dying around us. We were dying too, only a little slower. I was pulling a corpse, and I heard someone across the road in the women's tent camp say, "Tolek Chari?" There were several women's camps, and the blocks were so overcrowded that some were now sleeping in tents. Anyway, I didn't recognize her. She told me she was a classmate of mine—we graduated together in the ghetto. This old, emaciated woman in rags and I were the same age.

One night, I ended up sleeping next to a Russian prisoner of war. He was at the point where he couldn't sit up, hold the soup bowl, and feed himself. He was too weak. I tried to help him, but he wouldn't let me hold the bowl for him. He thought I was trying to steal his soup. He died that night or the next. I used his corpse as a pillow. That's how it was for several days—dirt and death, no food, no escape. The only escape was to be part of a prisoner exchange. Shortly after we arrived, I saw a group of Jewish prisoners marching out of the camp, headed for the train station. They were in civilian clothes, and some wore prayer shawls. We heard later they had passports from the so-called neutral countries and were being exchanged for German POWs.[99]

I did get out of camp one day. I went with a work group to the train station to clean out boxcars or something. I don't remember the task. I only remember that one prisoner ran for the forest. A guard fired and missed.

---

[98] A bomb knocked out the electricity that powered the pumping station. There was a stream nearby, but camp administrators made no effort to bring water to the prisoners. The daily rations at this time were down to ¼ liter of soup. Kolb, *Bergen-Belsen*, 43-46.

[99] Four transports, carrying a total of around 7,000 "exchange Jews," left Bergen-Belsen in early April, 1945, the first on April 6 and the others on April 11. Ben Shephard, *After Daybreak: The Liberation of Bergen-Belsen, 1945* (New York: Schocken Books, 1945), 18-19; Paul Kemp, compiler, *The Relief of Belsen, April 1945: Eyewitness Accounts* (London: Imperial War Museum, 1991), 6.

The prisoner kept running, straight to the trees. I remember watching and thinking he should zig-zag. I couldn't scream to the guy. I could only pray, "Don't run in a straight line. Weave. Fall down. Do something." He didn't. He was only ten or fifteen yards from the woods when the next shot killed him. So close.

Gelbart, the Sonder from Łódź, came even closer. A few days after we arrived, we started hearing heavy artillery and seeing flashes of light. There were fewer and fewer SS men in camp. The Germans were fleeing, and the only guards left were Hungarian and Lithuanian militiamen, and they were wearing white armbands to show their willingness to surrender. Prisoners could now go outside the barracks at night without fear of being shot. In fact, Heniek and I slept outside. We made a sleeping bag by buttoning our overcoats together—the front of one to the back of the other—and crawled in. We slept outside because, as the weather had become warmer, the barracks had become stickier and stinkier. And the warmer it was, the more the lice would bite. Our overcoats were full of lice, but we suffered fewer bites in the cool night air.

As awful as it was in the death camp, you could tell things were changing. One afternoon, Gelbart and I were hiding in a latrine, resting, avoiding work. There was a gap between the roof overhang and the top of the latrine wall. We were standing on the seat, watching through the gap in case a guard approached. I said something like, "Gelbart, we're going to be freed pretty soon."

"I don't know," he replied. "I have a pretty bad feeling."

"Gosh, they're wearing those armbands. It's practically over."

"I don't feel good about it."

The next morning, Gelbart was pulling a corpse when he saw prisoners pushing a cartload of rutabagas. This is what I was told. Gelbart ran over and grabbed a rutabaga. An SS man happened along on a bicycle and shot him. Gelbart had temporarily escaped on the walk back to Bergen-Belsen, and now this. So close. That afternoon, we were liberated.

We stopped pulling corpses around noon—I don't remember why—and went back to the barracks. No one told us to keep working. The Germans were gone. The militiamen in the guard towers were ready to surrender. We heard a rumbling coming through the trees from the highway. There was a lot of commotion. We rushed to the wire and...the guards didn't shoot. Someone said he saw a tank. Someone saw a US flag. And black soldiers. Then everybody imagined they saw them. The Americans were coming! It was wishful thinking.   Years later, I learned that German officers had arranged with the British to surrender a few miles of front line and the death camp.   They feared that, if there was fighting, prisoners would escape and carry lice and typhoid fever to nearby villages.[100] That same afternoon, three or four ambulances came inside the gates. We were happy, but there were no expressions of joy.   We were barely alive.   I remember the ambulances clearly—large vans with red crosses on the side. They drove through camp on the main street where a few hours earlier we had been dragging corpses. They had bullhorns. "YOU ARE NOW UNDER THE PROTECTION OF THE INTERNATIONAL RED CROSS." That was the end of the war for me.[101]

---

[100] The cease-fire around Bergen-Belsen was signed on the night of April 12, 1945. Most of the SS left the following day. British troops entered the camp on April 15. Kolb, *Bergen-Belsen*, 47.

[101] The standard account has British tanks passing by Bergen-Belsen on the morning of April 15, and a few British vehicles probably entered the camp. Later the same day, a British armored car equipped with loudspeakers entered Camp I and announced liberation. The following day, more British troops arrived and the armored car again toured Camp I, repeating the announcement. Joanne Reilly, *Belsen: The Liberation of a Concentration Camp* (London: Routledge, 1998), 23 and 150; Shephard, *After Daybreak*, 31-37. The Royal Army Medical Corps arrived on April 17 and the British Red Cross on April 23. Kemp, *The Relief of Belsen*, 7. Sington, *Belsen Uncovered*, 9-25, is the account of the British officer who drove the loudspeaker van into Bergen-Belsen on April 15.

6

A DISPLACED PERSON

The arrival of the Red Cross ambulances was good news, but good news doesn't fill your stomach. That evening, I went out organizing. There was a camp warehouse nearby, separated from the "death camp" by two barbed wire fences set about six feet apart. I suspected the warehouse contained food. Three or four days earlier, I had seen a prisoner crawling back under the fence from the warehouse. A young SS man—under twenty years old—also saw him and shot him from twenty yards away. The prisoner kept crawling. The second shot came from five feet away, and that ended it. This made no emotional impression on me. It wasn't unusual or shocking. We understood the penalty for going through fences. That's just how it was. However, after the Red Cross arrived, I wasn't worried about getting shot. I stepped through the fences—they had been cut—and went into the warehouse. Other prisoners were already there taking food. I grabbed three loaves of bread. I tied one in each pant leg and carried the third inside my coat, but not well hidden. I wasn't concerned about sneaking past guards, but the low-ranking functionaries might be a problem. They hadn't had a lot of authority—they cleaned barracks, kept registers, that sort of thing—but they did get more soup than the average prisoner and had more opportunity to organize additional food. Being better fed, they were physically stronger, and they were used to pushing other prisoners around. They were bullies. My hope was that, if they saw the loaf under my coat and took it from me, they wouldn't think to check my pants. Sure enough, some of the tough guys were waiting at the fence. I heard them say, "Looks like we've got some bread."

They were Polish, so I immediately began swearing in Polish, calling them awful names, showing I wasn't Hungarian and I wasn't intimidated. They said, "Hey, he's one of ours," and I kept my bread—all three loaves.

Back in the barrack, Heniek and I didn't tear off pieces of bread the way starving prisoners did. Already, our attitudes were changing. Heniek had organized some rutabagas and some sort of knife. We put slices of yellow rutabaga between slices of bread and called them "cheese sandwiches." We pretended it was normal food. We didn't save some for later, either. Each loaf weighed three or four pounds, and we ate all three.

The next morning, I was totally exhausted. I could barely stand up. All my nervous energy was gone. Two weeks earlier, I had walked all the way from Ahlem. Less than twenty-four hours earlier, I had been dragging corpses through camp. Now I couldn't walk one hundred yards. If a guard with a whip had been there, I would have found the will, but there were no guards anymore. And no whips. I had allowed my nerves to relax a little, and the exhaustion hit me. I managed to walk fifty yards to the end of the barrack, to the kitchen, and saw prisoners taking rutabagas from a pile in the storage area. I was practically in a panic, thinking, "What will we eat if they take all the rutabagas? What will be in the midday soup?" I had eaten rutabagas for so long, I couldn't imagine eating anything else. In Bergen-Belsen, when I dreamed about good food, it was a thick soup with rutabagas sticking out. People who have never been that hungry cannot comprehend being that focused on food. Today, looking back, even I can't comprehend it. It's like the fat judge chastising the skinny thief in the Daumier cartoon: "I too get hungry sometimes, but *I* don't go around stealing bread."

That second evening, British troops brought food into the camp.[102] It was something like pork and bean soup, thick and rich, a good meal for British soldiers, but impossible for starving prisoners to digest. We weren't accustomed to so much protein and fat. Our digestive systems lacked the enzymes to process it. They should have given us something like oatmeal. There were sixty thousand prisoners in the camp, and we all got diarrhea. Many died from it. Others recovered in Red Cross hospitals. I had constant diarrhea for several weeks, but wasn't sick enough for the hospital. However, for the next twenty-five years or so, I had "nervous diarrhea." If I started feeling hungry for as little as thirty minutes, my psychosomatic response was

---

[102] The British brought food and water on April 16, 1945. Shephard, *After Daybreak*, 38-39.

diarrhea. Of course, I don't blame the British soldiers. They brought us whatever they had and didn't know any better.[103]

Heniek was taken to a hospital and ended up recuperating in Sweden.[104] I didn't manage to locate him until 2005, sixty years after liberation. That year, a woman named Halina called me. She said she knew me from the ghetto. We had dated. She even knew where my grandparents had lived. But I had no idea who she was. She was three years younger than me, and I had been a Sonder and she had been a ghetto nobody, so if we had dated, it had meant more to her than to me. Halina told me that she was going to a meeting of survivors, and I asked her to try to find Heniek Krakowski. She knew of a Krakowski who had moved to Miami. When she called Miami, she talked to that Krakowski's widow, and it turned out that Heniek was the widow's brother-in-law. Halina called Heniek, then called me, and finally I was able to contact my old friend. That is how the survivors' network often worked. After two years in Sweden, Heniek had moved to the US and changed his name to Henry Crane. That's why I couldn't find him. He earned a master's degree in chemistry, eventually retired from an engineering job, and, when I called, was working as a consultant in New Jersey. It's hard to convey how close we were in the camps—sleeping side by side, looking after each other, sharing food when neither had enough. So much trust. Sharing food hadn't seemed extraordinary or heroic. It seemed natural. We kept each other going. Maybe we gave each other hope. Heniek—Henry—died in 2006. We never saw each other. We talked on the phone a few times, but he couldn't really recall the events from sixty years earlier. He didn't remember the lucky decisions on our first morning in the Bergen-Belsen mud. He didn't remember saving my life.

Besides bringing in food, the British soldiers got the camp water supply running again.[105] We immediately started cleaning ourselves. We made a fire, heated water in our soup bowls, and bathed. It took four or five bowls of water to wash your entire body. We didn't have soap, so we used sand to scrub away the dirt. One of the guys was a barber, and he fashioned a razor. He took a razor blade, which another prisoner had organized, inserted it

---

[103] It took the British soldiers two days to realize the survivors needed different food and even longer for the food to arrive. Lavsky, *New Beginnings*, 43. Some estimate that 2,000 died due to receiving the wrong food. Shephard, *After Daybreak*, 20.

[104] On June 19, four hundred left Bergen-Belsen for Sweden. Lavsky, *New Beginnings*, 59.

[105] At first, the British brought water in tanker trucks. On April 19, they had a pipeline running to a nearby stream. Lavsky, *New Beginnings*, 44.

through a split piece of wood, and tied the wood back together with string. It was like a tomahawk—the wood was the handle and the blade was exposed on both sides. The barber used it to shave our heads to reduce the lice. While I was looking for food in the warehouse, I came across brand new striped pajamas. I had never been issued a uniform. In all the different camps, I had worn tattered civilian clothing—whatever they gave us. I was happy to have this new uniform to go with my fresh haircut, happy to trade the dirty rags for something clean. The lice probably carried the rags away.

Our British liberators, too, were concerned about the lice. They dusted us with DDT powder to kill the insects. We were now clean, but we were still prisoners. The British kept us in the camp, under armed guard, because they didn't want us roaming the countryside. They feared we would spread typhoid fever or steal from German villages. I didn't have typhoid, but, once I was strong enough, I did go foraging. I snuck out past the guards—it wasn't difficult—and walked two or three miles until I came to a village. I went to a few farmhouses, and no one was around. They were probably hiding, thinking I was dirty, diseased, and dangerous. During the war, German civilians had been told that the people in camps were criminals. Well, I wasn't stealing, I was organizing. I didn't find much. I organized some eggs. I tried to kill a barnyard animal—a chicken or piglet or something—but the animal wouldn't cooperate. In a farmhouse kitchen, I saw a hand pump over the sink. The farm family could get water without going outside, without breaking ice off the pump in winter. That impressed me. An indoor water pump in a farmhouse. Such astounding progress. On my way back to camp, a British car came by. The soldiers could tell I was a prisoner, not a German, and they tossed me a pack of cigarettes. Not all British soldiers were like that. In fact, we didn't like the British guards. They acted like guards. When I re-entered the camp, one stopped and searched me. He was looking for fresh food for himself. Unfortunately for him, he was inexperienced at searching an experienced organizer. I opened my coat, allowing him to frisk my torso. He didn't find the eggs in my coat pockets.

At least the British didn't force us to drag corpses. They assigned that privilege to local German civilians and SS men. British soldiers used bulldozers to push thousands of corpses to the mass graves. The German workers tossed in corpses one by one. There were enough to keep them busy for days. Then they spread dry chlorine or lime on the corpses as a disinfectant. Before covering over the graves with dirt, the British brought in the *Burgermeisters*—the German mayors from nearby villages—so they could see what their countrymen had done, so they could no longer claim ignorance.[106] The British also made films of the camp, and civilians in the area had to watch the films before getting their ration cards properly stamped. There's a well-known picture of a mass grave at Bergen-Belsen. All the corpses are piled up, except one is leaning against the grave wall, near the top, almost like it's standing up. I remember seeing that corpse in that position. I remember tossing corpses into that grave before liberation. But, when I see that picture, I don't have an emotional response. It's just my life. Reading about current atrocities—that affects me more. I have some idea what those people might be going through.

Some time in the first week of liberation, I wrote a letter to my uncle Icchak, my mother's younger brother. He had moved to Israel in 1935 or 1936. He was the only close relative I had who was likely to be alive. The letter was basically a list of death notices—my grandparents, my parents, my aunts and uncles, my cousins. I was certain they were all dead. I wanted to let Icchak know what had happened to the family. He and I were all that was left. You could say I was also reaching out to the living, announcing that I was still here. Or maybe I just wanted food. I asked Icchak to send two grapefruits. What a treasure that would be! I gave the letter to the Red Cross. On the envelope, I wrote something like: Icchak Grabowiecki, a truck driver in Israel for Shell Oil before the war. That was the closest thing I had to an address. I never heard back from him. Later, though, I learned that he did indeed receive the letter.

A few days after organizing the eggs, I became a Czech. Or maybe it was a few weeks after—the chronology is hard to keep straight after so many years. The British were gradually evacuating the death camp. They sent the weakest prisoners to hospitals in Sweden and Germany. Most prisoners moved to the barracks at the nearby military training facility. This took some weeks.[107] There were thousands of prisoners to delouse, register, and relocate. I was anxious to get out of Bergen-Belsen, so when I heard that the Czech prisoners were getting ready to leave, I told the British that I was from Czechoslovakia. What I'd heard was the Czechs would stay in Celle, a town about ten miles away, until a transport to Czechoslovakia was arranged. I had no intention of being on that transport. I just thought the temporary

---

[106] It took two weeks to bury ten thousand corpses. Lavsky, *New Beginnings*, 44-45. The *Burgermeisters* attended on April 24, 1945. Shephard, *After Daybreak*, 74.
[107] The evacuation began on April 24 and was completed by May 21. When a barrack was emptied, the British burned it to the ground. Kolb, *Bergen-Belsen*, 49.

accommodations in Celle would be better than the death camp barracks. I was right. In Celle, they put us Czechs in a three or four-story military barrack.[108] Everybody had a bunk. There was plenty of food. We could come and go as we pleased. I found out that German Jews could register for ration cards at the Celle city hall, so I temporarily became a German. Other Polish Jews from Bergen-Belsen were doing the same thing. We claimed to be German Jews from Breslau, and the city officials gave us coupons for sausages and other food.[109] We had a joke: the suspicious registrar asked the Polish Jew, "*Sprechen Sie Deutch?*" The Polish Jew replied, feigning exasperation, "*A shale.*" That means "what a question," but it's Yiddish, not German.

After a week or so in Celle, the Czechs got on a train. I became a Pole again. I wandered around town, not sure what to do next, until I encountered a British medical unit. I told a medic I had a cough—which was true—and asked to be put in a hospital. He was unimpressed and showed no interest until I told him the cough was so bad I couldn't smoke. "What? You can't smoke?" I shared a room in the Celle hospital with a Russian POW. For the first time since leaving the ghetto, I had a clean, wide bed. After two weeks of rest, I was dismissed. I wandered back to Bergen-Belsen. The British had burned the concentration camp. I went to the military base which now housed many of the prisoners. Former prisoners. We were now officially Displaced Persons (DPs), and the military barracks were now a DP camp. I found a guy who had a room to himself, and I moved in with him.

I stayed in the DP camp at Bergen-Belsen for approximately two months. It wasn't terrible. There was food and other supplies. We could come and go freely, although British soldiers would sometimes search us to see if we were bringing in anything they might want. One guard took a cheap watch off my wrist. It you had something valuable, you had to sneak it in. Still, it was better than a death camp. Mostly, it was boring. Our only diversion was taking short trips. Small groups of us would walk to the nearby highway and hitch a ride with a German trucker. That was no problem. We went wherever the driver was going. The British had issued us DP cards, so we had no trouble passing through military checkpoints on the roads. We

---

[108] On May 8, 1,000 Czechs were transferred from Bergen-Belsen to Celle, followed later that month by 1,100 Poles. The Czechs were repatriated, but the Poles refused to return to Poland. Lavsky, *New Beginnings*, 58. Shephard, *After Daybreak*, 207-208, offers different dates and statistics.

[109] Breslau is now the Polish city of Wrocław.

frequently went to Braunschweig, a town about fifty kilometers away. Some Ukrainers lived near Braunschweig. They had probably been forced laborers during the war. Now they made vodka, which they traded for scarce goods, like the t-shirts given to us at the DP camp. Farther outside of town, there was a DP camp for about fifty Jewish women from Poland. They were in pretty good physical condition, not sick and emaciated. I think they had been working in a factory when the war ended. We went to Braunschweig for the booze and the women. There was a lot of screwing going on. One time I took the Braunschweig women some tampons—another scarce commodity. I organized the tampons from women in the Bergen-Belsen DP camp. They screamed at me and chased me, but I got away. We also went to Hanover. We knew some Łódźers there—the ones left behind in the Ahlem infirmary, and others who left the Bergen-Belsen DP camp and set themselves up in the Hanover black market. I found Sosiek, my relative, in a Hanover hospital, and he introduced me to a nice Jewish girl. A very cooperative Jewish girl. She was my first intimate partner after the war. By the way, some of the women in the Bergen-Belsen DP camp lived in what had been the German officers' quarters. There I found Hanka Kotlicki, my former girlfriend, and her sister, Uka. I visited them several times before they left for Israel, where their father lived.

I had one big excursion during the two months I remained at Bergen-Belsen. With two other guys, I hopped freight trains going north and ended up in Hamburg, which had been heavily bombed. Returning German POWs were also riding the trains. Lots of dislocated people were moving around Germany now that the war was over. In Hamburg—what was left of Hamburg—we walked by a movie theater with showcase windows. A doorman opened the door. We stepped inside and wandered down a hallway with more showcases displaying fancy clothes and jewelry. We kept walking and ended up at a nightclub for black marketeers and their high-class call girls. It was a large, dimly-lit, very elegant room. We had some money—I don't recall from where—and I wanted to go in. It didn't bother me that I was wearing striped pajamas and a Hitler Youth belt. My friends, though, were hesitant. They were embarrassed to be wearing rags in such a fancy place. I told them the Germans were the ones who should be embarrassed. It was the Germans who put us in *schmates*.[110] That's how it was. We went into the club and had a beer.

---

[110] *Schmates* is Yiddish for clothing in general, but also rags.

Later, we ate at an elegant restaurant on Alster Canal. I remember that it had portholes for windows because the water level in the canal would rise and fall. The food was very good—better than Bergen-Belsen rutabaga soup—but still only vegetables. You needed ration cards to get meat and fat, and this restaurant didn't bother with that. We also visited Hagenbeck Zoo, then noted for keeping animals in open-air enclosures rather than cages. The zoo had been damaged in the bombing, and it seemed like the animals didn't have their usual living arrangements and food. I felt sorry for them. I guess I momentarily forgot my own condition.

I was very impressed by the Hamburg city hall, a gorgeous building that somehow escaped the bombing. I went there to request an official certificate verifying that I had been in the camps. I'm not sure exactly why I did this. I hadn't heard of other survivors doing this. With my camp uniform, shorn hair, and DP card, it wasn't difficult to prove I had been a prisoner. I guess I figured a German certificate would eventually come in handy. And I wasn't afraid to demand things from the Germans—in city hall, a nightclub, or wherever. I was no longer afraid of them. I was starting to exchange my prisoner attitude for a new attitude: I survived, so fuck you.

I'll give you an example. I was taking one of the Jewish girls for a walk near Braunschweig, and she noticed a rose hanging over a garden fence. I broke it off for her. A German woman came out of the house and screamed at me. I just stood there.

"The wild times are over," the German woman said.

"For you," I replied. "For me, they're just starting."

She called a policeman, but he didn't want to get too close to a camp survivor. He stood at a distance and told me not to do it again.

Another time, a group of us—maybe six or eight DPs—got on a bus from the ladies' camp to Braunschweig, and we started singing the anthem from the Neuengamme concentration camp. I don't remember the words. I think it began, "Close to Hamburg there is a camp...." We were singing to aggravate the Germans on the bus. We felt we had a certain right to annoy them. We also refused to pay for the bus ride. DPs could ride the trains for free, and we extended that benefit to buses and streetcars. The way we saw it, the Germans transported us for free during the war, so why not now? If the bus driver argued or threatened to pull over, we still wouldn't pay. What was he going to do, send us to a camp? Eventually, the German passengers would shout him down, telling him to let us ride.

We spent three or four nights in Hamburg at a facility where German POWs, concentration camp survivors, and other returnees could get meals and a bed for a few nights. I heard some interesting stories. One German told me he spent twelve years in the camps before being liberated at Buchenwald. Twelve years! The Nazis had arrested him early on for being a communist. He survived for so long because the political prisoners were the upper-management at Buchenwald—they ran the concentration camp. Another German I met had been sentenced to death—twice. He was tall, very handsome, and clever. He had been sent to a concentration camp as a political prisoner, managed to escape, then was arrested for not having identification papers. Had they known he had fled a camp, they would have killed him on the spot. Instead, he claimed to be a soldier on leave who got separated from his military unit. This bought him some time while the Germans authorities determined that he was lying. When they sentenced him to death, he told them, "I want to die with a clear conscience." He confessed to having a Jewish girlfriend, though he didn't tell them she was hiding in Switzerland. This crime also required some investigation. Germans like accurate records. Eventually, he received a second death sentence. Then he confessed to a third violation—having children with the Jewish girlfriend. More investigation, more delay. Then he was released. A German judge freed him because of "the uncertain political situation"—the British Army was practically knocking on the door. The judge also announced his final sentence—two death penalties plus ten years in prison—"just in case the situation changes." In other words, if the Nazis regained control, the sentence would be enforced. The guy showed me the certificate with the sentence on it. He said that a few days after his release he introduced the judge to the British military police.

Before we left Hamburg, I rode a streetcar out of downtown to a suburb. The stores there still had clothing for sale, and I bought a light-blue dress shirt—my first new shirt since leaving the ghetto. I was so proud of that shirt—my one valuable possession. When we got back to the Bergen-Belsen DP camp, the Swedish Red Cross was arranging a transport to take sick DPs to Sweden.[111] I don't know if they would have taken me—I wasn't really sick—but I didn't bother applying because I heard you had to leave everything behind, even your camp clothes, and I wasn't willing to part with

---

[111] In July, 1945, Sweden accepted over six thousand survivors. Lavsky, *New Beginnings*, 59.

my new shirt. You see, I wasn't planning for the future. I hadn't been expecting a future. When someone asked my age, I would catch myself saying sixteen. That was my age when the war began, when my father was killed, when we moved into the ghetto. In the ghetto and the camps, I didn't think about my age, I thought about food. Now I was twenty-one and just living, happy to be alive, happy to have a new blue shirt.

In the summer, seven of us left the Bergen-Belsen DP camp and moved to Frankfurt in the American occupation zone of Germany. We didn't know much about Frankfurt, but it seemed the best option. We were tired of living under British authority. The French occupation zone was small and far away. The Russian zone was out of the question. The Russians would send me back to Poland, and there was nothing left for me there. Besides, compared to western Europeans, the Russians were backwards. Russian farmhouses didn't have indoor water pumps. In Poland, people hated the Germans with respect and the Russians with contempt. I didn't have big plans, I just wasn't going east. That left the American zone. Before the war, Jews in eastern Europe called America the "golden Medinah"—the kingdom of gold. That sounded good. We hopped freight trains until we reached Frankfurt. We knew the Americans had captured Hildesheim from the Germans, then handed it over to the British. We figured the Americans wouldn't give away Frankfurt since their headquarters were there.

My six companions called me *"Burgermeister"* because I could speak German with the locals and find out what was going on. I got that nickname in the DP camp. When we left for Frankfurt, we pooled our German marks. I carried the money and purchased food for the group. I was the *Burgermeister* and chief financial officer. In the Fritzlar train station, we saw a poster announcing that any returnees could get a free suit that day. I went to the city hall and explained that there were seven of us. Probably, I had our DP cards. They handed me seven coupons for suits and sent me to a warehouse—no questions asked. It seemed like Germans didn't want to offend camp survivors. It was probably a mixture of guilt and fear. They didn't know if we were dangerous, didn't know how we would react, what we might say. Mostly, they wanted to keep their distance.

Seven Polish Jews in brand new suits—matching grey jackets and pants—arrived in Frankfurt on a passenger train. A passenger train was a freight train with wooden benches inside cattle cars. Upon arrival, we went to a Jewish community center, and they arranged rooms for us in local hotels. We had arrived at the right time. A few days later, the United Nations Relief and Rehabilitation Administration opened a DP camp for Jewish survivors from the east.[112] The camp was in Zeilsheim, a suburb about twenty miles from downtown Frankfurt. My friends and I were among the first ones in. We received registration numbers four through ten. *Herr Burgermeister* was number seven.

Life in the new DP camp was like in the previous one—basically nothing to do. That's how I felt. No past, no future, and nothing to do. There were plenty of women to fool around with, but not much privacy. We were living in barracks, about ten guys to a room. After three or four weeks, I moved into an apartment. The DP camp was located right next to the company housing for an IG Farben factory. There were rows of two-story four-plexes—four identical apartments per house, each house the same as the next. I rented a small room from a German woman and her daughter who lived in one quarter of a house. I think the woman's husband was in a POW camp somewhere. I can't remember how I paid rent. Probably with food. We received ample food in the camp. The dining hall served dinner, and they distributed bread—white bread!—and fruit and other things for our other meals. Meanwhile, the Germans were faced with food rationing.

One day, David Ben-Gurion came to the camp to recruit Jews to move to Palestine.[113] He gave a pep talk, and a German orchestra played "Hatikva," the Jewish national anthem. His message wasn't very appealing. First of all, you had to smuggle yourself through Holland or Italy. The British occupied Palestine, and they weren't allowing people in—which didn't improve our attitudes toward the British. Second, if you made it to Palestine, you had to live on a kibbutz. That sounded like hard work. Most of us wanted to go to the US. The Americans were rich. At home, before the war, we didn't have toilet paper. We used old newspapers. Americans had toilet paper. Even their soldiers had toilet paper! American officers were well-dressed and sharp. To us, they were demigods from the golden Medinah. Who wants to work on an Israeli farm, or stay in Europe—we knew what that was like—when you can go to America and sweep up the money lying in the streets?

---

[112] The Allies founded the UNRRA in 1943 in anticipation of the problem of refugees and other displaced persons. By the end of the war, the UNRRA and Allied forces had established five hundred assembly centers in the British and American zones. Atina Grossman, *Jews, Germans, and Allies: Close Encounters in Occupied Germany* (Princeton: Princeton University Press, 2007), 133.

[113] Ben-Gurion visited German DP camps in October, 1945, as chairman of the Jewish Agency for Palestine. Lavsky, *New Beginnings*, 35.

It was hard not to like the Americans. They were taking better care of us than the British had and they were punishing the Germans. Eleanor Roosevelt visited the camp accompanied by US officers, who were treating her with great respect. I heard her say to an officer, "They've been in barracks long enough. Find rooms for them." Within a few days, the Americans had decided the DPs should live in the IG Farben housing.[114] I.G. Farben—the company that produced the gas for Auschwitz. The German residents would be forced out. Only their furniture could stay. What a reversal! We were no longer the *untermensch*. We were superior to the Germans.

Not only were we rising socially, some Jews were rising from the dead.[115] Right after I arrived in Frankfurt, I saw it happen. I jumped on the back platform of a streetcar. I remember I had my rucksack containing all my possessions on my back, so this was probably before the DP camp opened. Someone said, "Chari?" It was Alfred, the French head nurse and my protector from the Wüstergiersdorf hospital camp. I had lost track of him when the hospital camp was liquidated and everyone was transported to Bergen-Belsen.

"Alfred," I said, "you're dead." In Hildesheim, one of the doctors from Wüstergiersdorf had told Heniek and me that Alfred had died at the Gross-Rosen main camp. Now Alfred was resurrected, and we resumed our friendship. He often came to Zeilsheim and played cards with us. Eventually, he went to work for the Jewish city council in Frankfurt.

To find somebody alive was a surprise. We didn't expect anybody to have survived. It was too unlikely. Dorka Rabinovicz, who I considered my fiancé in the ghetto, didn't survive. I ran into her brother after the war, and he said that Dorka and her two sisters were taken from Auschwitz to Stutthoff, a real tough camp. "They didn't make it," he said, as casually, as matter-of-factly, as you might say, "I did the laundry." That's how survivors talked. Everybody had lost their families. Everybody had stories of unimaginable cruelty. You couldn't claim any special significance for your

---

[114] Prodded by the Harrison Report, which called for better treatment of Jewish DPs, in September, 1945, General Eisenhower authorized the seizure of German homes. Grossman, *Jews, Germans, and Allies*, 162-164.

[115] At the end of 1945, there were 70,000 Jewish DPs in Germany, including 45,000 in the American zone. Jews continued arriving from the east, and most of them went to the American zone, which, at the end of 1946, held 150,000 out of 180,000. However, Jews represented less than twenty percent of the DPs in Germany. Lavsky, *New Beginnings*, 35; Grossman, *Jews, Germans, and Allies*, 132.

loss. Or for your survival. Every survivor had a miracle, every survivor was a miracle, which made your own miracle unremarkable. And it was more than just luck. Every survivor had benefited from the help of others and from some degree of privilege. We all had organized extra food. We were all guilty of selfish behavior. That was the only way to stay alive. I resented the few DPs who talked like they were innocent in that regard. They had made it, they seemed to think, because they simply got lucky, or because God wanted them to live. Their own efforts had nothing to do with it. To me, that sounded naïve or stupid. Or maybe they didn't want to admit they survived at someone else's expense. For most DPs, though, it seemed best not to talk about the camps. It was difficult enough to acknowledge to oneself that what had happened was real. We kept our miracles to ourselves.

I should point out, though, that we didn't become truly aware of the enormity of the tragedy until many years later. Right after the war, we didn't know millions were dead. Nobody did—except maybe a few Nazis. We didn't know the extent of what had happened at Auschwitz, Treblinka, and other extermination camps. In the ghetto, I had understood that people were dying. However, it was not until thirty or forty years later that I realized how lucky I was, for example, to end up at Hildesheim, that those weeks were R and R compared to most camp experiences. Only then did I begin to understand how privileged and lucky I had been compared to most Łódź Jews.

If Alfred's reappearance was a surprise, the next resurrection was a total shock. I was playing cards with friends in Zeilsheim, and a new guy showed up and started kibitzing. He had just come from Łódź. Lots of people were coming and going—everybody was looking for somebody—so this guy wasn't unusual, but his last name was. I told him that my grandfather had a foreman with the same name in his Łódź leather shop before the war. "That was my father," he said. Then, with great excitement, he said something unbelievable. "You know, your grandfather is in Łódź. Your grandmother also."

I became very sick—not immediately, but soon. I don't know if the illness was related to this impossible news. I mean, I had believed that my grandparents, like all the elderly from the ghetto, had been gassed upon arrival at Auschwitz—I was certain of it—and now they were alive. Also, the guy told me where my Aunt Eva and Uncle Arek were living in Łódź. I had some family after all. I wanted to go see them, but I developed boils over my entire body, including a huge boil in my groin. I was admitted into the DP

Anatol Chari (far left) and friends in Zeilsheim DP camp, summer, 1945

camp hospital, which is where I met another Dorka. She was a nurse's assistant, and she had a miraculous story I think is worth telling.

In winter, 1944-45, sixteen-year-old Dorka and her older sister, Hala, escaped from a women's transport in Poland. They jumped off the train, which was taking them west from Gleiwitz, a subcamp of Auschwitz. Hala jumped first, then four or five other girls, then Dorka. The SS guards on the train started shooting. Hala was injured and several other girls were killed. The bullets missed Dorka and her friend, Mala, but a German patrol with dogs tracked them both down and sent them by train to Buchenwald to be executed. Luckily for the two girls, Buchenwald was a men's camp. The Germans decided the girls couldn't be killed there. They had to be executed at the women's camp in Bergen-Belsen. The Germans put Dorka and Mala on a passenger train to Celle. They rode in a separate compartment with two SS men and three Russian women who had escaped from a different transport out of Auschwitz. On the ten-mile walk from Celle to Bergen-Belsen, Dorka sat down in the snow and said, "Shoot me." Her shoes were heavy and wet. She was exhausted. The SS men didn't want to shoot her because then they would have to carry her body to the camp to account for it.

155

They convinced her to keep walking, and another girl exchanged shoes with her. They reached the camp in the dark, and the SS men left them in the shower at the women's camp. The functionaries who worked at the shower were Russian women, and they recognized the voices of the Russians who had arrived with Dorka and Mala. Another stroke of luck. They had been at Auschwitz together. The functionaries took the five new arrivals to the barracks, where they could blend in with the mass of prisoners and avoid execution. Dorka was smuggled *into* Bergen-Belsen.

Meanwhile, Hala, who had been shot while jumping from the train, managed to avoid recapture. The next day, a Polish railway worker found her, took her home, and nursed her somewhat to health. But he was worried. He normally lived alone. Anyone who saw Hala would immediately be suspicious. Neither of them was safe. Hala thought the janitor in her old apartment building, which her family had owned, might be willing to help. The railway worker snuck her to Sosnowiec, her hometown, and the janitor hid her until the Russians arrived. The chance of the one of the sisters surviving the escape attempt was almost zero, yet both made it, and by very different routes. That, to me, is the real miracle here. Dorka was saved by the strange logic of the camps and the kindness of other prisoners. Two Christian Poles risked their own lives to save Hala. Initiative, luck, and help, and you *might* have a chance. After the war, Dorka married Izio, the guy who squeezed through the window at Bergen-Belsen to join the lucky five hundred.

In the Zeilsheim hospital, the American doctors gave me penicillin, which wasn't generally available. It took about two weeks for the boils to disappear, and then I was released. By then, the camp residents had moved into the houses of IG Farben. The woman I had rented from was gone. I moved into a top-floor apartment with two of the guys I traveled with from Bergen-Belsen. Redheaded Jakob and I shared the "master" bedroom. Fat Josl had the small bedroom in the back to himself. There was also a kitchen area and a toilet. We used the furniture that the previous occupants were forced to leave behind.

In December, I went to Łódź to see my grandparents. I went with a transport of Polish prisoners returning to Poland. The train stopped in Pilsen, Czechoslovakia, and I remember paying for a meal with the accepted international currency—American cigarettes. There were only a few Jews on the train, including one guy who was also going to Łódź for a visit. We agreed to travel together. From Fabryczna, the Łódź train station, we walked ten or fifteen minutes through a park to Aunt Eva and Uncle Arek's apartment. It was a large apartment—probably three or four families in five rooms—practically across the street from my grandparents' old apartment where I had lived before moving to the ghetto. My aunt and uncle slept in the kitchen. I knocked on the kitchen door around two a.m.

"Who's there?" my uncle asked.

"Tolek. Open the door."

He woke up my aunt and said, "It's Tolek."

"You're dreaming," she told him. "Go back to sleep. Tolek is long dead." Then they let us in and we slept on the floor.

The next morning, I visited the Jewish community center or returnees facility—whatever it was. Somehow, the center had obtained records from the ghetto, and I found my stepmother's worker identification card.[116] I also found cards for Hanka and Uka Kotlicki. In the afternoon, I went to see my grandparents. They were out in the suburbs, in a big summer house they had owned before the war. I took a street car, then walked a mile or so to their house. There weren't any telephones, so they weren't expecting me. I walked in, and Grandmother almost fell over. She had assumed that her three daughters, including my mother, and her two grandchildren hadn't survived. She was right about all but me. That evening, my grandparents told me the story of their own survival. We didn't really discuss my story. Mine was an everyday miracle. Theirs was truly remarkable. It was impossible. To begin with, they should have been gassed upon arrival at Auschwitz. Grandmother was over sixty, Grandfather over seventy, and the cut-off was usually forty. In the ghetto, Grandfather had protected Grandmother by keeping her "employed" in the leather factory. When the ghetto was evacuated, the leatherworkers traveled as a "closed group"—there were two train cars just for them—because they were deemed "essential" to the war effort. My sixty-year-old grandmother was an "essential" worker. It's true—the Germans couldn't have lost without her. Eva and Arek were also in the leatherworkers' transport, as was a distant cousin of mine—a two-year-old—who died of diarrhea in Auschwitz.

My cousin Chaim, who worked with electrical appliances in a ghetto factory called Schwachstrom Ressort, also went in a closed group. He told me that when the electrical workers got off the train in Auschwitz, they

---

[116] Hinda Chari's identification card is now held in the Museum of Tolerance in Los Angeles.

showered separately from the other prisoners and received new striped uniforms and blankets. Veteran prisoners told their group leader that a man from Siemens was in camp, looking for skilled workers. If he asks, "Can your workers do this?"—tell him yes, they advised, no matter what. They will take your group to a Siemens factory and, if you can't do the work, they'll train you. But when the Siemens agent asked the question, the group leader stupidly said no. The guards took away everything—the blankets, the new uniforms—and the closed group was dispersed into different work assignments like the rest of the prisoners. Chaim ended up in "Camp D," part of Auschwitz II, doing demolition work, like taking apart old aircraft. That's why, when I was in the adjacent "Gypsy Camp," he was able to toss me a piece of aluminum to use as a spoon.

The Łódź leatherworkers weren't assigned jobs in Auschwitz. They were held in reserve, in case leatherworkers were needed. Grandfather did repair shoes for privileged prisoners, like block leaders, kapos, and kitchen workers. In exchange, he got a better place to sleep, didn't have to carry the toilet bucket out in the middle of the night, and received extra food. Every evening, he would take an extra soup to Grandmother. They were in Auschwitz I, in a "semi-family" camp—women and children in one area, men in the adjoining area, with a wire fence in between. Grandfather handed the bowl of soup through the fence—it was only electrified at night—and this extra food helped keep Grandmother alive. One evening, while Grandfather was waiting for Grandmother at the fence, an SS man came by on a bicycle. He asked Grandfather what he was doing by the fence, what was in the bowl. "He hit me so hard," Grandfather recalled, "that I fell and spilled the soup— and Frume counted on me bringing her the soup." For him, in telling me the story, it wasn't worth mentioning that he lost hearing in one ear completely and the other ear partially due to the beating. The only thing worth mentioning was the spilled soup.

The Germans evacuated Auschwitz with death marches.[117] When prisoners fell in the snow or lagged behind, the SS guards shot them. The march was too much for Grandfather. Already before the war he had kidney problems. After three or four hours of marching, he fell and blacked out. When he regained consciousness, he was lying on a sleigh with five corpses.

---

[117] On January 18 and 19, in sub-zero weather, the SS marched 58,000 prisoners out of Auschwitz. Soviet trrops reached the camp on January 23. Raul Hilberg, *The Destruction of the European Jews* (New York: Holmes and Meier, 1985), 3:983.

The SS men must have decided not to waste a bullet on a dead man. Grandfather dragged himself to a barn, and the next morning the Russians arrived. Meanwhile, Grandmother survived the evacuation thanks to slow communication between the SS in Auschwitz and the Gestapo and *Sicherheitdienst* in Berlin.[118] The SS decided a group of about fifty older women, including Grandmother, were not capable of marching or being transported. I've read that it took two days before the SS received orders from Berlin to shoot the women. By then, the Russians were very close. As Grandmother described it, "They took us out of the block, and as we were walking down the road, a truck came from the opposite direction. The men in the truck stopped and spoke to the SS guards. The guards got in the truck and drove off, leaving us alone. We just kept walking. We knew what was behind us. We came to a large hole. That was probably to be our mass grave. We went farther, to the abandoned SS barracks, and found some cans of food. We lay down in the beds, and a day or two later the Russians arrived." Like I said, all survivors had miracles. The guards should have shot Grandfather when he fell. If the Russians had been a little slower, Grandmother would have ended up in that mass grave. They survived by miracles, and then were reunited in Łódź. I think it was Grandmother who returned first. She went to the Jewish community center and posted her name on a list. Two or three days later, Grandfather arrived and found her.

They were probably the oldest Jews to survive Auschwitz. They had to be. But Grandmother never fully realized what Auschwitz was. After the first shower upon arrival, when they were getting their clothes, Grandmother asked for a handkerchief. The sauna workers just pushed her out of the room, preventing her from drawing more perilous attention to herself. But when Grandmother told me about it, she complained about the rough treatment. "They were so rude to me at Auschwitz!" She was that naïve. She couldn't believe there was something like an extermination camp. She couldn't comprehend that such organized sadistic behavior was possible. She only knew something bad had happened, and it destroyed her religion. She said, "If my daughters didn't come back, there is no God." This was the woman who, in the ghetto, had tried to make pork "kosher."

I only spent one night with my grandparents, then returned to Eva's apartment. I had gone to see my grandparents, not to live with them. My grandparents' two-story house had ten rooms. They could only afford to heat

---

[118] The *Sicherheitdienst* was the SS espionage service.

**Anatol Chari's grandparents, Frume and Rafal Grabowiecki,
after the war—likely the oldest Jews to survive Auschwitz**

two of them. In their excitement at my appearance, Grandmother prepared a special meal for me. She opened a can of preserved meat. It was inedible. In Zeilsheim, we wouldn't have used it for cat food. Compared to Germany under the Americans, Poland under the Russians was miserable. Russians were not rich. Outside Eva's apartment, I saw a Russian soldier with bandages wrapped around his ankles because he had no socks. That was typical. He was rolling a cigarette with newspaper and Machorka, the lowest quality of tobacco. It smelled awful. This was no place for me. When I returned to the city, two guys recognized me from across the street and called me over. We knew each other from the ghetto and exchanged greetings. They had worked pushing carts in vegetable distribution. Then a third guy said, "Hey, he was a Sonder." It was dangerous if someone denounced you. The Russians sent some Sonders to Siberia as punishment for cooperating with the Germans. Fortunately, the other two stood up for me. "Be quiet," they told my accuser. "He was a decent guy."

I was happier about meeting Sabcia. She had been one of the privileged girls in the ghetto, and often came to my get-togethers. Before the war, her father had owned one of the biggest bakeries in Łódź. It was on Piotrkowska, practically across the street from our apartment. In the ghetto, her father was put in charge of a bakery, which meant Sabcia stayed well-fed and well-dressed. She could trade extra bread for whatever was available, like the nice clothing brought in by western European Jews. Sabcia was very attractive. She survived Auschwitz because, immediately upon arrival, she acquired a protector—a privileged prisoner who was able to move about camp. When I arrived back in Łódź, somebody must have told me that Sabcia was also there. I found her and agreed to take her with me to Germany.

I remained in Łódź for about a week. I was anxious to leave Poland, to get away from Russian authority, but it took some arranging and wasn't easy. There were three of us—Sabcia, me, and the guy I had met on the train to Łódź. I went to Piotrków, a nearby town, to pay some Jewish guys to procure official permits to leave Poland, signed by the mayor or somebody. Then the three of us boarded a Russian military transport to Berlin. The train was so crowded that Russian soldiers were hanging on the outside. In Zbąszyń, a town near the German border, the Polish military police took us off the train to make room for soldiers. They picked us because we were Jews. They said our official papers were worthless and ordered us to report to an office the next day. We got lucky. The officer we reported to was Jewish, and he said we could cross the border.

We were now five—two other Jewish guys had joined us. While we were waiting for the next train to Berlin, we overheard someone remark, "A Jewish girl wants to cross the border and doesn't want to give her ass?" We got out of there right away. The Polish border guards would have raped Sabcia. Rather than cross the border there, we took a train to Szczecin, a harbor city near a different border crossing. We found a Jewish home to stay in and arranged to cross the border in the back of a Russian freight truck. Two Polish plainclothes policemen showed up and demanded money. Everyone was part of the smuggling operation, everyone had to be paid. At least this time it was only money. The truck took about twenty passengers, including us, through the border checkpoint and on to Berlin.

We weren't home free yet. The western Allies controlled the western sectors of Berlin, but the city was deep in the Russian occupation zone of Germany. We made it to a gathering place for Jewish refugees in the British sector of the city and waited several days for the Jewish Brigade.[119] Acting independently of British authority, they were using stolen British trucks to smuggle Jews out from under Russian control. We wouldn't have to pay them. They were motivated by Jewish nationalism, not money. One night, we were awakened—"Hurry. The trucks are here." When I got downstairs, my traveling companions were already in the back of a crowded truck and the tarp was pulled down. I tried to climb in.

"We're full," a Jewish soldier said, and pushed me back.

"*Amchu*," I said quickly. In Hebrew, that means "I belong to the tribe." It was a Jewish password. Only a fellow Jew would know what it meant. The soldier reached down, grabbed my shoulders, and pulled me into the truck. We took the autobahn, which was open to international travel, through the Russian zone to Braunschweig or Hanover. Crossing into the British zone was no problem—we were in an official British vehicle after all.

I remember one more incident from the trip. We took trains the rest of the way to Frankfurt. When we crossed into the American zone, on a cold night, everyone had to get off the train. American soldiers were checking IDs. A German soldier, returning from a POW camp, grumbled or said something about the inconvenience. A US soldier got nose to nose with him and asked, "Who won the war, you or us?" That really impressed me. The German didn't reply.

My grandparents made it out of Poland the following year. That wasn't a miracle, but it helped to have some connections. Grandmother had a niece named Bobcia Solomian, who was studying in Sweden when the war began. She returned to Poland and served as a nurse among the partisans, twice escaping from a Gestapo jail. At the end of the war, she held the rank of first lieutenant in the Polish army and was awarded the Order of Polonia Restituta.[120] After the war, she married another Jewish officer. He had spent the war in a German POW camp for officers. They both went to work for the Polish government. She was some kind of undersecretary of education. He was an undersecretary of state for the Middle East. When Poland had another outbreak of anti-Semitic violence, Bobcia and her husband, both in

---

[119] The Jewish Brigade was an independent Jewish unit, fighting under the Zionist flag, in the British Army in 1944-1945. Abraham Hyman, *The Undefeated* (Jerusalem: Gefen, 1993), 42n23.

[120] *Order Odrodzenia Polski* or Order of Poland Reborn, one of Poland's highest honors.

uniform, drove Grandmother and Grandfather to Berlin.[121] From Berlin, my grandparents moved to Israel. My grandfather died a few years later, but, in 1959, I took my three-month-old son to see my grandmother. Bobcia and her husband were assigned to Israel twice—he as consul general—and the second time they declined to return to Poland.

Back in Frankfurt after my trip to Łódź, it was back to life as a DP—no past, no future, nothing to do. I was still living with Fat Josl and Redheaded Jakob, and now we also had Jakob's cousin, Little Josl, who slept in the kitchen. Little Josl was much younger than me. He was probably nine or ten when the war began. During the war, we were often in the same place at the same time. He survived the ghetto, despite working in a "4711" *kommando*— human waste disposal. At Kaltwasser, he managed to escape from the room holding the boys who were being sent back to Auschwitz to be gassed. He and I were on the same transport to Bergen-Belsen, and he, too, was among the lucky five hundred who went to Hildesheim and Ahlem. In fact, he helped pull Izio through the barrack window when the lucky five hundred were registering. Yet I never knew Little Josl existed until he moved in with us in Zeilsheim.

We also had German girls living with us. They were typically homeless refugees from eastern Germany. They slept with us and did the cooking. We gave them food and a place to stay. While the DPs in the American zone were well cared for, many Germans had trouble finding sufficient food. At a dance hall one night, a German guy asked if we were looking to meet women. He offered to introduce us to his sister and her friend if he could get a free dinner out of it. That's just how it was. Thanks to the Americans, I was back to having some privilege.

There really isn't much more to say about my six post-war years in Germany. The previous five years of war had been eventful, to say the least. Things were happening then, whether you liked it or not. After the war, except for finding my surviving relatives, not much happened, at least not to me. For a year and a half, my life was monotonous and non-productive. Mostly, my friends and I just sat in camp, in our apartments, and played cards. In the camps during the war, we hadn't thought about the future. We had lived moment to moment. The only thing to think about was how to get a little more food or an easier work assignment. Other than that, you had no

---

[121] The re-emergence of Jews in Łódź society was reversed, and many Jews fled west, after the pogrom in Kielce, Poland, on July 4, 1946. Grossman, *Jews, Germans, and Allies*, 162.

decisions to make, no control over the situation. You weren't responsible for yourself. In some ways, for me, life in the DP camp was the same. Now the American occupation forces and the UN were responsible for my well-being. They weren't telling me what to do and when to do it, but they made sure my basic needs were met. Some DPs worked in the kitchen and barracks to earn a little money and to organize additional food. I wasn't interested. I had enough to eat, and we could choose from a warehouse of used clothes donated by people in the US. Food, clothing, an apartment, and girlfriends— what more did I need? I remained stuck in some of the camp mindset—not terrorized, of course, not constantly focused on immediate survival, but still totally dependent and not thinking beyond today. I had no motivation to create a future for myself, or even to imagine one—until I read a romance novel.

I was friends with a DP named Jerzy Mines, who we called Jerzyk. He told me how, as a prisoner, he had worked in a Bussing truck factory in Braunschweig. The head cook at the camp had been a short-tempered German. He would get angry and hit a prisoner, then feel sorry and tell the prisoner to come to the back door of the kitchen in the evening for an extra soup. This happened one time to Jerzyk, and it gave him an idea. He figured the cook wouldn't remember who he hit each day and probably couldn't tell the prisoners apart anyway. Jerzyk went to the back door every night, pretending the cook had hit him that day, and got an extra soup. That's taking the initiative. One night, though, the cook eyed him suspiciously. "I didn't hit anyone today," the cook said, and that was the end of that trick.

Jerzyk tried to convince me to show some initiative. Other DPs had started taking classes at the university in Frankfurt. There was no reason not to. Jewish students were admitted without rigorous entrance exams. They didn't have to pay tuition and they didn't have to join German students in clearing the bombing rubble from the university campus. Jerzyk knew I had the Matura certificate from the ghetto school. He said, "You're the only one who's really qualified for university, and you're the only one not going." I didn't care. I was just lazy. I enrolled in a locksmith program offered in our camp by ORT, a Jewish educational organization, but quit after a few weeks.[122] I didn't find door locks particularly interesting. I did, however, frequently take the train to Munich to visit Eva and Arek. In 1946, they had

---

[122] ORT, founded in 1880, comes from the Russian words *Obshestvo Remeslenofo zemledelcheskofo Truda* (The Society for Trades and Agricultural Labor).

moved from Łódź to Berlin, and then to Munich. I liked to visit them because Eva prepared nice meals for me. My roommate, Jakob, encouraged me to go because Eva would always bake a cake for me to take back to Zeilsheim. Anyhow, I was there around Christmas, and I read this romantic story about a poor German boy whose girlfriend's family wouldn't accept him because he was uneducated. After he earned a doctorate, the family's attitude changed. The novelist made the point that in life, every once in a while, you get the opportunity to move up the ladder. If you let the opportunity go by, the ladder is taken away.

When I returned to Frankfurt, I immediately enrolled in the university. This was at the end of 1946. I enrolled in philology—general nothing—because that was the easiest way to be admitted, then immediately switched to medicine. That would be my ladder. Jerzy was also studying medicine. He said, "I'd rather work in a white coat than dig ditches." I knew about digging ditches from my time in Kaltwasser and Ahlem, so the white coat looked pretty good to me too.

In summer, 1947, I decided to switch from medicine to dentistry. Without the war, I probably would have ended up in law or journalism. When I was a kid, that's what I was interested in. I especially hated the thought of being a pharmacist or a dentist. I didn't want to stand behind a counter and count pills all day, and I didn't want to smell the breath coming from a mouthful of rotting teeth. President Truman changed my attitude, at least about dentistry. He announced a four-year period of unrestricted immigration to the US for refugees from eastern Europe, from behind the Iron Curtain.[123] You only needed a sponsor in America. I didn't want to go right away. I didn't speak English. I didn't know any Americans. I figured I wouldn't have much of a future in the US unless I arrived there with a useful education. It would have taken me five years to complete medical school in Frankfurt, by which time Truman's window would be closed. Dental school would only take three and a half. When I went to apply for admission, the place seemed empty. I didn't realize there was summer vacation. I wandered around until someone in a white coat asked what I was looking for. He was a

---

[123] Truman's presidential directive, on December 22, 1945, called only for preferential treatment of DPs, particularly orphans, under existing immigration quotas. The DP Acts of 1948 and 1950 allowed for much greater immigration. The Truman directive did allow voluntary organizations to sponsor refugees. Leonard Dinnerstein, *America and the Survivors of the Holocaust* (New York: Columbia University Press, 1982), 112-114, 168-175, 285-287; Hyman, *The Undefeated*, 416-419, 425-428.

sympathetic man, from an anti-Nazi family, and dean of the dental school. He asked for my application papers. This may have been another bit of luck. There were limited openings, but it helps when the dean personally delivers your application to the entrance committee. I suspect they thought I had his endorsement. Maybe I did. I got in.

Studying dentistry is how I met Mumpitz. Her given name was Margarethe, but she went by Gretel, and we called each other Mumpitz, which means something like "goofy." During the first semester, she and I were dissecting the same brain. I invited her to study with me in Zeilsheim. We studied all night long. She was a German girl, but she didn't need my food. Before the war, her father had joined the Nazi party, otherwise the Nazis would have confiscated his construction company. He wore a swastika, she said, "the size of a dinner plate," yet he sent his daughters to a convent school because he didn't want them infected with the Nazi propaganda taught in public schools. In the DP camp, I had enjoyed a steady stream of girls. That ended when I met Mumpitz. She was my girlfriend for the next four and a half years.

At some point, a woman came to the DP camp to recruits students to move to Israel. She had studied in Vienna and held two doctorates. When she interviewed me, I told her I wanted to earn one of my own and then I would think about living in Israel. She said something like, "With an attitude like that, you shouldn't have survived the camps." The truth is that I didn't consider myself a "displaced" person.[124] I didn't think of Poland as my homeland. It didn't feel like home. I felt more at home in Germany. I had a place to stay. I had an address. The woman did convince my friend Maniek R., the guy who fixed my electricity in the ghetto, to move to Israel. He became head of Nazi crime investigations, and later helped me locate my cousin Chaim, who was living in Israel.

Toward the end of 1948, the Americans began liquidating DP camps in Germany. Many DPs had already moved out. The Americans closed the smaller camps, including Zeilsheim, and sent the remaining DPs to a few larger camps. If I remember the dates correctly, Fat Josl had left for the US in 1947, and Redheaded Jakob followed soon after. Those of us still in the Zeilsheim camp were unhappy about the closure. We had it pretty good and

---

[124] The UNRRA defined a "refugee" as someone fleeing from home and unable to return. A "displaced person" meant someone uprooted by war, but expected to go home. Lavsky, *New Beginnings*, 17.

didn't want to move. Some guys even protested, claiming that the camp "synagogue"—a single-story building designated as a house of prayer, but heavily unattended—was a holy place. The Americans weren't impressed. When the camp closed, I rented a room in a large, second-story apartment across from the train station in the Nied district of Frankfurt. This was late 1948 or early 1949. The room was cold and unpleasant. Likewise, the landlady. Later, I heard she committed suicide. I was unhappy there, so after a while I rented a room in the third-floor apartment of an older couple. They were much warmer, very friendly. On Saturdays, I only had a half day of classes. I would get home in the early afternoon, and the woman of the house would have a big meal prepared for me. After the meal, she would say, "Judche ate his belly full and will sleep now." "Judche" meant "my dear little Jew." It was very affectionate, not anti-Semitic. I stayed there for the rest of my time in Frankfurt.

Despite living in a German home and having a German girlfriend, my privileged status was in decline. In 1946, I had traded two loaves of bread to a hungry German guy for a stolen 350 NSU, a German military motorcycle. But when the Deutschmark conversion, in 1948, allowed Germans to buy sufficient food, our DP camp rations lost their great exchange value.[125] I was no longer a rich guy. Then the DP camp closed. Being a camp survivor or eastern refugee no longer brought special attention. As life in Frankfurt normalized, as my life normalized, I became just another foreign student at the university. There was one new benefit, though. Frankfurt is in the state of Hessen, and the Hessen government, as part of a program of restitution, decided to pay Jewish survivors five Deutschmarks for each day spent in a concentration camp. I'm not sure of all the details. I only know that Jewish students at the university began receiving fifty Deutschmarks each month, with the balance to be paid upon graduation.[126]

---

[125] In June, 1948, the western Allies converted the German currency from the Reichsmark to the Deutschmark, and every German under western occupation received forty DM. The reduction of US occupying forces and the stabilized currency reduced the supply and demand for black market goods. Grossman, *Jews, Germans, and Allies*, 252.

[126] The 1953 *Wiedergutmachung* agreement did not provide for personal compensation from the Federal Republic for eastern European survivors. However, some compensation was already being provided at the *Länder* (federal states) level. Lansky, *New Beginnings*, 26.

Anatol Chari (right) in metalworker training, Zeilsheim DP camp, 1946

Anatol Chari and Aunt Eva in Munich, 1948

I had one other source of income. At Zeilsheim, my friends and I had traded a little in the black market.[127] At first, it was minor stuff, like selling some of the herring we received in our camp to DPs in the Bamberg camp. Nobody cared about that. Later, though, the operation became more delicate. Little Josl and I bought cigarettes and coffee—the main contraband—which had been stolen from the DP camp or American warehouses. Then we resold it to Germans in Frankfurt. This was real coffee, not the substitute stuff, and it was in demand. I remember a couple of encounters with the German police. One time, we put a fifty-pound sack of coffee in a small truck. The German police had no authority in the DP camp, but they could stop us once we left the camp, and this time they did. A policeman inspected the truck. He let us go, though, because Little Josl had bribed him in advance. On another occasion, we arranged to sell several cartons of cigarettes. When we arrived in the evening to make the delivery, the police were there to arrest us, only they had no evidence. We hadn't trusted the situation and had left the cigarettes behind. We were only selling a little here and there, but we did make enough money to buy an Adler automobile, which we used as a taxi, shuttling people between the DP camp and the nearest train station, in Höchst. I still have my first driver's license, dated 1946. Later, Jerzyk and I bought an Opel convertible. I think it was 1949 when Jerzyk lost control on an icy road, wrecking the car and almost killing us. After surviving Bergen-Belsen, that would have been an ironic way to go.

As black marketeers, Little Josl and I were small potatoes compared to my Uncle Arek. I'll put it this way: Arek always knew how to take care of himself. Before the war, he and Eva had owned a leather goods store down the street from Grandfather's store. When the ghetto was liquidated, Arek smuggled money and a diamond into Auschwitz. He used the money to buy privileges and, when Auschwitz was liquidated, he possessed several hundred cigarettes. And he still had the diamond. At roll call one time, during an inspection, he dropped it and kicked dirt over it, then recovered it later. After the war, Arek began operating in the Berlin black market. This was serious business. When it became too dangerous, Arek and Eva moved to Munich. The first time I visited them there, Arek was in the hospital with tuberculosis. Pretty soon, though, he was involved in a smuggling operation that sent silver to Milan, Italy, and brought back silk scarves. Arek and his partners paid US

---

[127] Before the currency reform of 1948, the black market may have represented over half of all economic activity in Germany. Hyman, *The Undefeated*, 291-291.

officers, who could cross the border without customs inspection, to transport the goods.

Beginning in 1948 or 1949, sometime after I had moved in with the nice couple, Little Josl and I began working with Arek. We drove to Munich, filled our car with thousands of scarves, and sold them to German stores in Frankfurt, earning three or four cents per scarf. This wasn't particularly dangerous. The German police weren't concerned about silk scarves the way they were about stolen American cigarettes and coffee. As a full-time student, I was trying to make ends meet. Often, I was broke. One night, I dreamt that my father gave me a little money. Before I got out of bed the next morning, I heard someone down in the street shouting, "Chari! Come downstairs!" It was Alfred. He had smuggled in some wool cloth from Paris and wanted me to sell it for him. He gave me five dollars for my trouble. Another time, he brought me some material for a camel coat for Mumpitz. I wasn't trying to be a businessman. I just had some opportunities once in a while. One December, heavy snow closed the passes between Italy and Germany, making it difficult to bring in Italian goods. I told Arek to get all the scarves he could. During the holidays, there were gift stands in the Frankfurt streets, and I sold enough scarves to the stands that Christmas to cover my living and university expenses for the year.

Arek played cards with David Gertler, the guy who had been Sonder chief in the ghetto, the one who had decided not to fire me, the one who allowed me to get my own apartment. Contrary to the joke told in the ghetto, Gertler had not ended up in a can of pork. The Germans took him to Auschwitz, and stuck him in "The Bunker," a cellar jail where prisoners were punished with isolation or held awaiting execution. He got enough to eat because he worked for the Jewish prisoner in charge of the jail. After six months, he was released into the Auschwitz I camp, where a block leader recognized him as the Sonder chief and beat him almost to death. Moise Hasid, the Jewish criminal prisoner in charge of the sauna—the guy who held up my riding boots—stopped the beating and put Gertler under his protection. That's the story Gertler told me, anyway. I met him at Arek's home in Munich and thanked him several times for saving my life. He downplayed it. He just said that he had known my father before the war. "Your father," he added, "probably went to Gleiwitz." I doubt it was true. I think Gertler may have been trying to ease my mind, giving me a lie to live on rather than me not knowing anything at all about what became of my father.

Dental school students, ca. 1948
(Anatol Chari far right, "Mumpitz" third from right)

I suspect my father died in the Radogoszcz prison, not in a concentration camp, but I'll never know for sure.

In October, 1950, I took my last dentistry exam, and in December I defended my dissertation, which compared the morbidity and mortality of DPs in German camps to the general German population under Western occupation. Because I was a DP, the Americans had allowed me access to the medical archives. I was now a Doctor of Dental Medicine. I went to Munich for the holidays so that Aunt Eva could proudly introduce me as "My nephew, the doctor." After dental school, it was no problem finding an American Jewish organization to sponsor my emigration to the US. In fact, they were looking for us, perhaps to assuage their guilt for not having done more during the war. The Hebrew Immigrant Aid Society (HIAS) took me. However, I didn't go for almost another year. I worked in the emergency room of the university dental clinic until Jerzyk finished medical school. Then together we arranged passage on an American troop transport ship, the

BESCHEINIGUNG

Es wird hiermit bescheinigt, daß

Herr
Frau   Anatol C h a r i
Frl.

in   Frankfurt/M

geb. am 8.6.27 zu Lodz

i. d. Zeit vom: 1.5.40 bis: 14.4.45

n dem KZ-Lager / ~~Zuchthaus / Gefängnis / Gestapogefängnis~~ *)
Ghetto: Litzmannstadt
~~KZ: Auschwitz, Groß-Rosen, Bergen-Belsen~~

inhaftiert gewesen ist.

Er (Sie) gilt somit als politisch, rassisch und religiös Verfolgte(r).

Diese Bescheinigung ~~~~, ~~~~ gewährt~~~~ Sonder- oder
Vorzugsrechte gemäß den Vorschriften der amerikanischen Militärregierung.

Ministerium für pol. Befreiung
für das Land Hessen
Im Auftrag :

Wiesbaden, den 10. 11. 1948.

*) Nichtzutreffendes streichen.

**Postwar certificate, verifying ex-prisoner status
(original in Holocaust Museum in Washington, D.C.)**

172

General Taylor.[128] As doctors, we would work in the ship's clinic as needed, but wouldn't have to clean the deck and do other chores.

Before we left Germany, Jerzyk and I went to a government office in Wiesbaden to request the balance of our restitution payments. A secretary told us the checks weren't ready, the money wasn't available.

"We're leaving soon," I told her. "We need to get our money now."

"If you're not nice," she scolded me, "you might not get it at all."

Jerzyk and I didn't hesitate. We sent straight to an interior minister's office. He was out, but we met his deputy, Mr. Oppenheimer.

"This is Dr. Mines," I said, "and I'm Dr. Chari." I told him what had happened with the secretary. He picked up the telephone.

"Dr. Chari and Dr. Mines are here," he told the secretary. "I'm sending them over to pick up their checks."

A few minutes later, the checks were waiting for us on her desk. Like I said earlier, there are two sorts of people—those who stand before desks and those who sit behind them. I refused to remain stuck in front of the desk.

Jerzyk and I arrived at Ellis Island on October 10, 1951. I had $5.25 in my pocket. I bought two pears on the pier for five cents each. I was in the golden Medinah.

---

[128] From 1950 to 1957, the Navy used the USNS *General Harry Taylor* in the Military Sea Transportation Service. It was later called the USNS *General Hoyt S. Vandenberg.*

POSTLOGUE

Of course, Tony Chari's story didn't end at Ellis Island. When he and Jerzyk presented themselves at the HIAS office in New York City, a woman there turned to Jerzyk and said something like, "You as a physician are nothing here." To Tony she said, "You as a dentist are absolutely nothing." We sponsored you, she was saying, but don't expect too much. Their professional degrees from Germany wouldn't be accepted outright in the US. Before he could practice medicine, Jerzyk had to serve an internship and pass boards—which he did. A foreign-trained dentist had to attend dental school for at least two years to learn American dentistry. Tony attended the University of Iowa School of Dentistry, became a US citizen, then served in the US Air Force in Turkey for two years. Beginning in 1960, he undertook graduate training in periodontics at the University of Alabama-Birmingham and served a residency in the Veterans Administration hospital in the same city. He opened a practice in southern California in 1963, taught periodontics at Loma Linda University, USC, and UCLA, and retired from practice in 1985. Today, he lives in Laguna Beach. Twice married and twice divorced, he has two children, two grandchildren, and two girlfriends. Deuces wild!

Celebrating final exam, Frankfurt, 1950, in Palmengarten, at the time a US officers' club (Anatol Chari third from left, "Mumpitz" third from right)

Anatol Chari (second from right) with Jewish university students on excursion to Mainau Island on Lake Constance, 1949

Anatol Chari (left) with friend at Königssee in Bavaria, 1950

**Anatol Chari (on Mercedes 170) with longtime
friend J. in Frankfurt-Nied in summer, 1950**

ADDENDUM

Tony's struggle with German authorities had one final reprise. In 1991, Tony contacted the Bundesversicherungsanstalt für Angestellte (BfA), the German social security program, to apply for pension benefits. After all, the German government had considered Łódź part of the Reich during the war, and Tony had worked for the Łódź gasworks, a company that, under German control, should have paid into the social security system on behalf of its employees. The Social Security Agreement, signed by the US and West German governments in 1979, seemed to establish pension rights for German refugees living in the US. In 1993, Tony received notice that his application had been rejected. At one point, the BfA had required that he appear for an interview at the German consulate in Los Angeles in order to prove that he was either ethnic German or had been brought up in German culture. However, they now argued that he was not eligible for a German pension because the Łódź gasworks company had not paid into the system on his behalf. Tony retained a German lawyer to appeal the decision in a Berlin court, but little came of it.

In 1996, a new US-German Social Security Agreement went into effect, this time specifically granting benefits to people who had lived in parts of Eastern Europe that Germany took over during the war. In April, 1997, with the BfA still denying his claim, Tony sent a letter to the office of the German chancellor, Dr. Helmut Kohl, requesting help in the matter and pointing out that SS men, who fought so heroically against the Jews, were receiving pension payments while their Jewish victims were being denied. The spirit of the Reich lived on, he said. The chancellor's office could have simply ignored the letter or informed Tony that individual pension cases were not a matter for the chancellor's office. But instead, someone in the office was concerned enough to forward Tony's letter to the Bundesministerium für Arbeit und Sozialordnung (Ministry for Labor and Social Order). "You will hear from them," the chancellor's office promised. And he did. The chancellor's office was not without influence. In May, the Ministry informed him that his case was both being reviewed by the Bundesversicherungsamt, the agency that oversaw the BfA, and under consideration in the court which adjudicated pension disputes. The Ministry expected to receive reports on the progress of the case, but did not want to give the impression of trying to influence the outcome of the dispute. A Ministry official must have taken a careful look at Tony's file, however, because he wrote an extensive letter defending BfA practices and explaining how former SS members were carefully investigated and evaluated before their pensions were approved.

In August, the Ministry informed Tony that they had learned from the Bundesversicherungsamt that the BfA had rejected his appeal. However, it seems that even as the BfA continued to resist the US-German agreement, Ministry officials were staying involved—perhaps due to the interest shown by the chancellor's office. Indeed, the Ministry assured Tony that the Bundesversicherungsamt would continue reviewing the case. Then, in mid-September, the BfA informed the court in Berlin (Sozialgericht und Landessozialgericht) that they had changed their decision on Tony's case. According to their letter to the court, the BfA now had a new understanding of the 1995 US-German agreement, and for the first time ever they would allow "subsequent contributions." In other words, Tony would now receive his pension as if he had contributed to the system while employed by the Łódź gasworks, but the BfA would deduct from his benefits the amount that should have been contributed at that time. Put another way, even though during the war German government officials, directly or indirectly, killed Tony's father, forced his family from their homes, required that they live and work as prisoners in the ghetto, failed to make the appropriate payroll deductions from Tony's meager ghetto wages, then used him as a slave laborer before dumping him to starve in a death camp, the BfA was insisting that Tony, some fifty years later, was still responsible for the missing payroll deductions. In one final bureaucratic nicety, the Bundesversicherungsamt, on October 7, sent a letter to the Ministry, claiming credit for the BfA's new ruling. In the end, in 1998, after seven years of what he calls "bureaucratic chicanery," Tony began receiving monthly pension payments from the BfA. This included back payments, plus interest, dating to December 1991, when he would have become eligible, and the missing contributions were not deducted. Later, the Berlin court ruled that the payments should date back to July 1990.

Crossing the Atlantic on USNS General Harry Taylor, 1951
(Anatol Chari top, Jerzyk middle)

Captain in US Air Force, 1948-1950

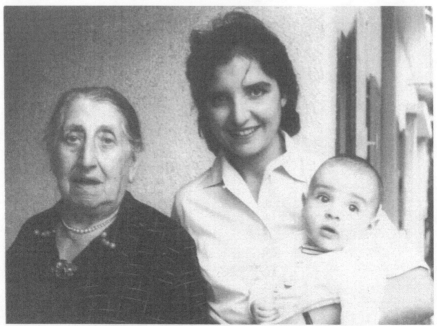

Anatol Chari's grandmother Frume, his first wife Nota,
and their three-month-old son, Peter, in Israel, 1959

POSTSCRIPT TO THE ENGLISH EDITION

In 2009, quite by accident, Tony learned of a victims memorial in Radogoszcz, a suburb of Łódź, where a Gestapo prison once stood. In January, 1945, the day before Soviet troops arrived, the Germans set fire to the prison, killing hundreds of Polish prisoners. This was also the prison where, at the start of the war, the Germans held prominent Łódź citizens, including Tony's father, Councilman Piotr Chari. In 2010, at age 87, Tony visited the memorial, still believing he would never know the circumstances of his father's death. The entire story of the Holocaust will never be told. But in the museum at the site, Tony received a warm and enthusiastic reception, and a docent named Wojciech Źródlak located a file card documenting Councilman Chari's incarceration. Tony learned that prison conditions had been brutal, and that the Gestapo used a truck which the prisoners called "the hearse." The truck usually arrived once a week and transported prisoners to nearby Lućmier forest, where the Germans executed them. The museum archives contained the dates of these mass murders. Most likely, "the hearse" came for Councilman Chari on November 23, 1939, thirteen days after his arrest. Despite the passage of seventy years, this information left Tony, in his words, "emotionally disturbed for two or three days."

Anatol Chari at Radogoszcz memorial, 2010

DP

www.lunycrab.com

Made in the USA
Charleston, SC
11 December 2011